Perfect
Recruitment

THE PERFECT SERIES

ALL YOU NEED TO GET IT RIGHT FIRST TIME

Perfect Recruitment

ALL YOU NEED
TO GET IT RIGHT
FIRST TIME

DAVID OATES
and VIV SHACKLETON

ARROW
BUSINESS BOOKS

Published by Arrow Books in 1994

1 3 5 7 9 10 8 6 4 2

First published by
Arrow Books Limited
20 Vauxhall Bridge Road, London SW1V 2SA

Random House Australia (Pty) Limited
20 Alfred Street, Milsons Point, Sydney
New South Wales 2061, Australia

Random House New Zealand Limited
18 Poland Road, Glenfield
Auckland 10, New Zealand

Random House South Africa (Pty) Limited
PO Box 337, Bergvlei, South Africa

Random House UK Limited Reg. No. 954009

ISBN 0-09-937921-X

Set in Bembo by
SX Composing Ltd., Rayleigh, Essex
Printed and bound in Great Britain by
Cox and Wyman Ltd, Reading, Berks

ACKNOWLEDGEMENTS

The authors would like to thank the following for their help in compiling this book:

Miles Broadbent, chairman Norman Broadbent; Nigel Broome, senior manager, retail personnel, Sainsbury's; Julian Burnett, PA Consulting Group; Dr Robert Edenborough, principal consultant, MSL Human Resource Consulting; Liz Harrison and Ron Eldridge, Saville & Holdsworth Ltd.; Alannah Hunt, Price Waterhouse; Patricia Marshall and Charles E. Bethell-Fox, Hay Group; Adrian Savage and Richard Scriven of ADS Veliger Ltd.; Ian Veltman, chairman, Hoggett Bowers; Ian Lloyd, managing director of MSL International; and Simon Whan, managing partner, Learning Curve.

ABOUT THE AUTHORS

David Oates is a freelance business journalist who contributes regularly to management journals and the business pages of the national press. He has written or coauthored six management books, including most recently, *Leadership: The Art of Delegation* (Century Business) and *The Manager as Coach* (FT/Pitman). Prior to turning freelance, he was managing editor of *International Management*, a magazine circulating to senior executives worldwide. In 1985 he received the Wincott Award for a series of articles about the management of small firms. A Fellow of the Royal Society for the Encouragement of Arts, Manufactures and Commerce (RSA), he is married, has three daughters, and lives in Devon.

Dr Viv Shackleton is a chartered occupational psychologist, a university lecturer and a consultant to business. He is Senior Lecturer in Work Psychology at Aston Business School, Aston University, Birmingham, and has held university appointments in the United States and continental Europe, as well as in Britain. He is author or co-author of four books and numerous articles. His most recent books are *How to Pick People for Jobs* (Fontana) and *Successful Selection Interviewing* (Blackwell). As Senior Partner in his own consultancy firm, Shackleton Consultants, he advises companies on setting up recruitment and selection systems and on the management of people. He is married and lives in Warwickshire and London.

CONTENTS

INTRODUCTION

Perfect recruitment means getting the right person for the right job every time. It means never having to say 'Sorry, I made a mistake' or 'Pity, but that appointment just didn't work out'. It means never having to sack someone for incompetence. It means never having to accept someone's resignation because they have found a better job. Perfect recruitment means that the person and the job suit each other to perfection.

Yet as everyone knows, perfection is an impossible dream. Nothing in this world is ever perfect. None of us is ever going to get it right every time, especially where human beings are concerned. I fondly remember the story I heard some years ago of the distinguished professor of business psychology who had made a name for himself helping companies recruit and select the perfect candidate. He was asked to advise an international company on the appointment of a finance director. Two years later that finance director upped and ran off with several million pounds of company money. He was last heard of somewhere in Argentina. Yet I know for a fact that the famous professor continued to ply his trade of advising companies on their recruitment and helping them select the best. And why not? Everyone knows that you can't predict with perfection. Even the best, most highly acclaimed and amply paid consultants, who have spent a lifetime recruiting people, are oh-so fallible.

All you can do is reduce the odds of making a mistake. That is what this book is about. It sets out the steps which lead along the path to the discovery of an excellent new recruit. It is a guide towards perfect recruitment.

The first step is to know what you are looking for, and

is covered in Chapters 1 and 2. What does the job entail? What is the culture of the organization that the success-ful candidate will join? What are the skills, aptitudes, attitudes and qualities required in such a candidate? These days these skills and qualities are likely to be called the necessary 'competencies' for the job. But you need to consider not just the competencies required now. Organizations and the jobs they contain are changing at such a rate that the job demands are unlikely to be the same in a few years time. Unless you want to fire and start again, you had better consider what these changes are likely to be, and whether a key competency isn't the ability and willingness to change and adapt along with them.

Then comes finding the candidate. This would seem easy in the days of high unemployment. But fishing in the right pool to get a good catch, but not so large as to get overwhelmed by the weight of applicants, is the trick. Like all tricks, it is easier said than done. Should you use a consultant to help you get a shortlist, or are you better advised doing it yourself? Chapter 3 will help you decide.

Selection is often the most difficult aspect of the re-cruitment process. These days there are tests, assess-ment centres, statistically analysed application forms, structured interviews, panel interviews, work samples, and numerous other gizmos to help (or further confuse) the bewildered. Chapters 4 to 7 set out the pros and cons of each method and help you make choices about which ones would suit you.

Finally, there is the follow-up and the post-mortem. Specialists are fond of saying that recruitment is only one part of the successful management of people. It's true. Perfect recruitment won't solve all your prob-lems. The problem may not even be recruitment. I was once asked to help select a sales director for a small firm. The company had appointed three previous sales directors, each of whom had lasted only a year or so. The company believed that they were recruiting the wrong sort of person. It soon became obvious that this wasn't the problem at all. The explanation for the turnover of good people was that the existing directors had not been able to accept the 'upstart' onto the board. They had their well-tried ways of doing things and each new recruit had rocked the boat. Each new sales director had tried to set the sales policy and move the organization forward, but had been blocked by the 'old guard'. Team building for the new board, efforts to induct the newcomer, a build up of trust and mutual learning were required, not better recruitment.

Perfect recruitment is like professional gambling. Many of us have a flutter once or twice a year. We stake 50p each way on the Grand National and choose the horse because we like its name or the jockey smiles a lot. We usually lose. The professionals study form. They look at the course, the conditions of the turf, the jockey, the horse, the track record, the length of the race and which type of race a particular horse prefers. Then they make a calculated guess. They don't get it right every time, but they make a better job of it than we amateurs. This book aims to make you more of a professional when you place your bets on your favourite candidate. It should help to make you an almost perfect recruiter.

Viv Shackleton

SPECIFYING THE COMPETENCIES

The perfect recruitment campaign starts with drawing up the specifications for the perfect candidate. No such paragon may exist, but identifying the qualities you are seeking in your ideal applicant gives you a goal to aim for.

Essentially recruitment involves two important issues:

- What do I want this particular job-holder to contribute to the organization?
- What sort of person will be best suited to make a success of the job?

Traditionally, recruiters have often answered both those questions by looking at the previous job incumbent and trying to find someone of similar skills. Experience shows, however, that simply looking for a clone of the last job-holder is too limiting.

Times change and so do the requirements of a job. The way the job has been done for the past five years will almost certainly be inappropriate to the way it should be done today and over the next five years. What you really need is someone who will take the job forward and expand it into areas that break new ground.

Moreover, jobs change. In the late 1980s, a study of managerial mobility found that more than half of the jobs to which managers moved were new, either in whole or part.

However, there is likely to be a number of common denominators shared by the existing job and how it should be carried out in future. The starting point for many experienced recruiters is to arrive at a job description as a result of a thorough job analysis.

JOB ANALYSIS

Job analysis is the process of collecting and then analysing information about a job. It should include the context in which the job is performed and the tasks and responsibilities involved. This provides the basis for the job description.

Many recruiters ignore job analysis altogether. They move straight into the job description. This is unwise. Job analysis is the foundation stone of successful staff selection. Without it, you cannot know what you are aiming for when assessing candidates. It is like shooting in the dark.

Methods of job analysis

There are four major methods of analysing jobs:

- interviewing
- questionnaires
- observation
- diaries

Interviewing. The interview is conducted with existing employees. It is designed to reveal the nature of the work so that you know what the new job–holder's responsibilities will be. It also looks at how the job is changing and is likely to change in the near future.

Questionnaires. Employees describe their jobs by answering a series of questions about what tasks or activities they perform, how often they do them, how important they are and so on. A future orientation can also be built in to the questions, but changes are more difficult to pinpoint than with interviews.

Observation. Staff are observed as they carry out their job. (Sometimes they are videoed.) Information is recorded and analysed about the types of activity they perform.

Diaries. Here employees record their own activities in a work diary or log book. The analyst then uses the diaries to learn about the nature of the work.

An efficient job analysis should cover a number of key aspects:

1. company culture
2. the nature of the job
3. the medium-term challenges
4. the skills needed to match the job
5. the reward package

1. Company culture
Some recruitment experts insist that job analysis should include an awareness of an organization's culture. Indeed, some maintain it is the foundation of job analysis. The first exercise that the search and selection arm of PA Consulting Group carries out when called in by a client is to examine the whole organization – and that can include the parent company if the organization in question is a subsidiary – to understand something about its history and its ethos.

The argument is that the marketing director of an established business selling well-tried products, for example, is a totally different animal from the marketing director of an entrepreneurial start-up company.

PA uses an organization 'values and style' questionnaire to help clients describe, through a series of prepared statements, the kind of organization they operate in. Culture mismatch is probably one of the main reasons why someone appointed to a new job doesn't make the grade, despite having all the right qualifications.

The appointee, for example, might be used to operating very autonomously, whereas the new company culture is one where the corporate rules have to be strictly adhered to. Equally, the appointee may have a lone-wolf operating style, whereas the new company culture is one of team working and group decisions.

2. Nature of the job
Having identified the company culture, the next stage is to isolate the key elements of the job to provide the fundamental benchmarks when interviewing the candidate. This should be the acid test of whether the candidate is going to meet your job requirements. Can this person help you, for example, to create additional sales through a new sales channel? It is basically defining the *raison d'être* of the job.

There are clearly some practical dimensions of the job that have to be considered, such as the amount of assets to be controlled and the number of people under the job-holder's supervision. Job applicants will want to know those details anyway. Nevertheless, the main issue is whether the person applying for the job will be able to make things happen to achieve the goals of the organization.

3. Medium-term challenges
Most applicants will be able to do the standard job. A financial controller will be able to prepare budgets, for example. But the key issue, where job analysis is concerned, is the candidate's ability to cope with the medium-term challenges of the work.

The recruiter needs to identify what the medium-term challenges of the job are; then answer the question of whether the job applicant is the sort of person who is likely to be able to get to grips with them. Rather than looking for a teacher who is proficient and stimulating in the classroom, you may need to look for administrative skills to assure yourself that he or she can cope with the increasing amount of paperwork. Rather than looking for a secretary who is proficient at routine tasks you should perhaps be seeking one with the ability to introduce electronic diaries or arrange an international management conference.

For the financial controller it could be the negative goal of maintaining costs within budgets. Or it could be phasing in a new IT system. If the financial controller hasn't done it before, he or she could have serious problems.

You should identify medium-term challenges through which the job-holder is going to make a substantial difference to the organization. Out of that and an examination of your company culture and the *raison d'être* of the job will emerge the skills and qualities of your ideal applicant.

4. The skills to match the job

So the skills and qualities flow from the earlier analysis – but what do they look like? Here is a sample list taken from the job of an area sales manager for a motor manufacturer:

Communication Skills:
  – Oral
  – Formal presentation
  – Written

Analysis & Judgement:
  – Verbal
  – Numerical

Building & Maintaining Relationships:
- Negotiation
- Commercial Awareness
- Strategic Thinking etc.

Each skill should be defined in behavioural terms so that it can be assessed at the selection stage. So Commercial awareness might have seven or eight key indicators including:

- Awareness of threats and major opportunities in the market place (e.g. competitors, changing customer perceptions and needs).
- Keeps up-to-date with latest developments in all relevant fields by establishing networks, etc.
- Relates decisions to corporate objectives (e.g. uses corporate objectives as criteria for decisions).

5. The reward package

When considering the rewards to offer for a specific job, recruiters often think only in terms of money – salary, bonuses and share options. However, money is often not the main motive for people changing jobs. Indeed, if the job applicant is only interested in money, you will need to ask yourself how long he or she is likely to stay with you after the appointment. Will you get your investment back if the successful applicant leaves within two or three years, enticed by a more lucrative offer?

By only thinking in money terms you are also restricting the range of people who could possibly bring benefits to your organization. People seek a new job for a whole host of reasons other than more money. It might be that they are seeking the chance to exercise autonomy, the chance to move into a larger organization or, conversely, the chance to work in a smaller firm. It could simply be that they want to move to a more rural location or they are fed up with their current boss.

When arriving at the reward package, you should think

of other aspects. What are the psychological rewards, as opposed to the material rewards, that make your organization and the work on offer an attractive proposition that is going to entice someone away from their present job?

PERFORMANCE CRITERIA

There is a growing view that job analysis is insufficient in itself to arrive at the qualities necessary to perform a specific job. Some experts argue that there is an inherent weakness in the job analysis approach – that the inferred links, between what a job demands and the personal qualities that will supposedly enable a job-holder to meet those demands, are typically based as much on faith and the experience of the job analyst as on any empirically demonstrable connections.

Even when the personal qualities identified by the analyst are the right ones, this guarantees little. It is very difficult, just by looking at job content alone, to identify which of the qualities listed are particularly important in producing superior as opposed to merely acceptable job performance. Hay/McBer, the behavioural-competency division of Hay Management Consultants, has developed a technique for identifying the personal qualities needed for jobs.[*]

The method begins not by focusing on the content of the job, but rather by specifying clearly what it is that the job should deliver as output. In other words, the method takes as its starting point job *performance* rather than job *content*. So the first step is for the organization to examine the position to be filled and answer a simple question: 'What are the performance criteria for the new job-holder that we would use in deciding whether or not we had hired the right person?'

[*] Bethell-Fox, Charles E., Hay Group UK, 'Competency-based Recruitment and Selection', Chapter 3, *Competency Based Human Resource Management*, Kogan Page, 1993.

In a production job the main criterion might be 'Produce X amount of Product Y to Quality Standard Z, by Time T'. In a service job, it could be 'Provide effective answers/solutions to clients' needs/problems promptly and courteously'. In a sales job 'Sell X amount of Product Y by Time T with less than 5 per cent customer complaints and more than 40 per cent repeat business'. And for managers, whether of production, sales or service, 'Manage a group of people who achieve Productivity Level X to Quality Standard Z by Time T', as well as some planning and strategic outputs at more senior management levels.

Person specifications

The job description relates to what the job-holder does or is expected to do. The person specifications tell you what are the main characteristics of successful job holders. You then know what qualities to assess in candidates.

This is the area of recruitment that has given rise to considerable debate in recent years. Several factors have combined to cause a shift of emphasis in the qualities many companies look for in a successful job applicant. The term 'competencies' is often used in this context to describe people's ability to perform certain functions, either technical or inter-personal, such as being a team leader.

Transferable skills

According to Philip Schofield, writing in a November 1993 issue of *The Sunday Times*, a revolution in the way people and jobs are matched is under way. When recruiting people, says Schofield, employers used to look mainly at qualifications and experience in similar jobs. Many now realize that jobs have two components – knowledge and skills – and that skills, or competencies, acquired in one role are transferable to others.

Schofield makes an important distinction between knowledge and skills. Knowledge, he suggests, is gained from academic or professional education, or informally, through experience. Skills are more about *how* people do things. While knowledge may be specific to a particular job, skills tend to be generic and can be acquired in areas other than work.

Core skills – team working, oral and written communication, listening and counselling skills, leadership, problem solving, business awareness, setting priorities, managing time effectively, numeracy and computer literacy – are valuable in any role. Because these have universal application they are usually called 'transferable skills'.

BEHAVIOURAL CHARACTERISTICS

Hay/McBer sees skills and knowledge as the tip of a competency iceberg (see Figure 1.1). Below the surface of the iceberg the consultancy lists four behavioural characteristics which all serve to motivate people at work:

- social role
- self-image
- traits
- motives

Skills and knowledge are at the peak of the iceberg, above the surface. On the first level below the surface is *social role*. This drives behaviour through an understanding of what the role requires in a social setting and that is where managerial drive starts to impinge. Underneath that there is another level which also drives behaviour and that is *self-image*, the kind of mental picture that a person has of himself or herself. Research shows, for example, that those with a positive self-image perform better, have higher expectations and

9

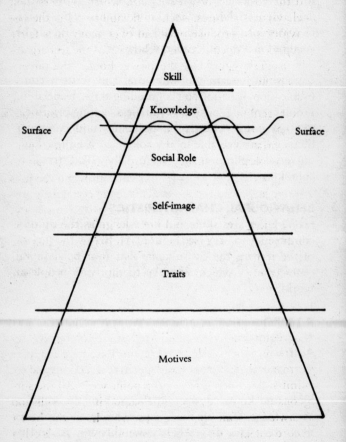

Fig. 1.1 *Hay/McBer's Competency Iceberg*

match themselves to jobs more accurately than those with a lower self-image.

At the next level down are *traits*, which are persistent behavioural features, such as flexibility. It is the behaviour you produce over and over again. It is fairly deeply embedded. Down at the base of the iceberg are the *motives*, which are the power-house, the unconscious motivators.

Most recruitment and selection in the past has been conducted above the waterline of Hay/McBer's iceberg, concentrating on skills and knowledge. A lot of emphasis was placed on CVs. 'What can you do?' 'What do you know?' 'Let's look at your education and the jobs you've held.' Skills and knowledge are certainly a prerequisite of any job. You cannot be a surgeon if you don't know how to open somebody up and take out the right organ. Nevertheless, Hay/McBer insists that the characteristics below the waterline are the ones that make the difference between mediocre and superior performance.

THE ROLE OF THE SURGEON

The consultancy has conducted some interesting research into the role of the surgeon. Based on such performance indicators as post-operative infections and re-admissions, they illustrate the point well. All the surgeons in the survey have the same kind of skills and knowledge. But the surgeons who have the better record construe their role as somebody who heals other people (social role). The self-image relates to somebody who actually helps other people to help themselves. The traits are about empathy and care and the motive drive is empowerment of other people.

The surgeons with a record of patients with more post-operative infections and re-admissions construe their role as an expert and see themselves as somebody who knows better than the person they are dealing with. They are often characterised by aloofness. They talk about 'the kidney on Ward 3' and they are actually driven by achievement. They count their successes according to the number of operations they perform and the slickness with which they carry them out.

HARD AND SOFT SKILLS

Recent management trends have caused a shift of emphasis away from technical skills towards inter-personal skills. One of these influences is *empowerment*, the trend towards devolving authority to the employees closest to the customer. This is bringing about a funda-mental change in the role of the manager – and in the contribution of front-line employees.

Managers are having to switch from the old command and control mode of operating to one in which they become more of a coach and facilitator. It is very hard for managers schooled in the traditional authoritarian style of management to make this radical change. In-creasingly, organizations are relying on the recruitment of new blood to change the managerial climate.

This means that recruiters are emphasizing the 'soft' skills of people-handling over the 'hard' technical skills that used to predominate in job advertisements. The theory is that it is much easier to teach technical skills than it is to train managers to change their entrenched behaviours.

Each organization must, of course, decide for itself the balance of skills it is looking for. What is certain, is that unless you make an inventory of the competencies you are looking for in job applicants, it will be an almost im-possible task to recruit the calibre of staff that is most appropriate for your organization.

Generic

That said, it is widely recognized that there are a large number of similar jobs in the world and that there is a high degree of commonality about the competencies required to perform those jobs. This has led occupational psychologists and professionals in the field to arrive at a range of generic skills to fit these standard jobs. For example, the five most commonly identified management competencies used by graduate recruiters in the retailing industry are:

- *Self-confidence and personal strength.* Candidates should be confident, self-motivated, resilient and able to exercise emotional control.
- *Leadership and teamwork.* Candidates should be capable of playing an active and effective part in a team or group as both a leader and a subordinate.
- *Planning and organization.* Candidates should be capable of establishing the most appropriate course of action to accomplish a specific goal by effective management of resources.
- *Analytical and problem-solving skills.* Candidates should demonstrate effectiveness in analysing situations, identifying issues; focusing on possible problems and gathering relevant information.
- *Human relations and influencing skills.* Candidates should be capable of taking actions which demonstrate their impact on others within the immediate work environment and take account of the feelings and needs of others.

The ideal graduate recruit, sought by retailers, is confident, a good team player, analytical, organized and able to sell both ideas and products.

Off-the-shelf

The recognition of generic skills has led to the formulation of a number of 'off-the-shelf' frameworks or plans which loosely fit the requirements of a standard job. Of course no job is exactly the same in two organizations. Every company needs to adjust the general template to its own specific needs. The standardized plans nevertheless provide a framework to build on and reduce the amount of basic research an organization has to undertake for itself.

Establishing the norms

A number of companies have arrived at the qualities they are looking for in job applicants by conducting in-depth analyses of their existing talent – trying to isolate the competencies that have helped their staff to develop successful careers. Another popular approach is to compare high performers with average performers. This helps to pinpoint the qualities that make the difference between a run-of-the-mill performance and the performance of someone who really helps to move your organization forward.

It is important, however, to supplement these historical or present-day pictures with some 'guestimate' of how the world is moving. So you may need to build in, for example: capacity for self-knowledge, behavioural flexibility, listening skills, openness to new experiences, networking (to discover what others are doing and thinking), interest in self-development (assuming these are not already in the analysis) to try to make people 'future proof'.

There are problems. Nobody knows the future and competencies are notoriously difficult to measure – but the attempt should be made if today's successful managers and organizations are not to become tomorrow's dinosaurs.

Critical Incident

Another widely used approach is to focus on a critical incident. The rationale is that the qualities which distinguish excellent from mediocre performance show up most clearly at those critical, make-or-break times of crisis. You, therefore, sit down with someone in your organization and get them to recount a number of critical incidents he or she has been involved in. The incident can be positive or negative. It can be an event that led to a good result or one that led to a bad outcome. Exploring these events and how the person behaved in coping with them should hopefully reveal key qualities needed to tackle difficult moments.

Repertory Grid

A more sophisticated approach is provided by a technique called the repertory grid which aims to distinguish people by isolating their views, attitudes and understanding of the world around them. By using repertory grid interviews it is possible to compile a hierarchy of people's views, from the issues that they feel most strongly about to those which they consider are only of minor importance. These views can then be related to a particular job. Analysis of the results calls for a high degree of skill, however, and should only be done by an experienced psychologist.

MORE LIKE ME

Inexperienced recruiters often fail to do any research into the qualities they are looking for in a prospective job holder. They tend to look for people in their own image. The similar-to-me effect is a well-established principle in psychology. It has been shown, for example, that the higher the perceived similarity between supervisors and their subordinates, the higher the performance ratings they assign to one another.

This tendency often occurs unconsciously. Recruiters think they are assessing people fairly and objectively but they are in fact biased by the all-too-human tendency to like people who are similar to themselves better than those who are dissimilar. It can also happen at a conscious level. Recruiters rationalize to themselves that they are pretty good at their job, so someone exactly like them will fit the bill nicely.

The dangers of this approach are all too obvious. Recruiters taking this view might not of course be as good as they think they are. Even more importantly, the qualities that make that person good at his or her job may not be those required for the particular vacancy that needs to be filled.

KEY POINTS

- Draw up specifications for ideal job candidate
- Arrive at a job description
- Take account of company culture
- Pinpoint key elements of the job
- Identify medium-term challenges
- The reward package is broader than money
- Examine job output as well as content
- Make an inventory of the competencies the job requires
- Look for transferable skills
- Behaviour characteristics indicate superior performance
- Be aware of 'hard' and 'soft' skills
- Generic skills can be found in all jobs
- Compare high performers in your organization with average performers
- Look for long-term potential.

FINDING THE CANDIDATE

Once you have decided on the type of candidate you are seeking, the next stage is to attract the attention of the right calibre of applicants. You have two choices – do you do it yourself or do you employ someone to do it on your behalf?

There are a host of professional recruiters prepared to take the task off your hands – for a fee of course. But let's first of all assume you are going to tackle the exercise yourself.

The least expensive method to attract candidates is simply to spread the word around. One well-known company used to pride itself that it never advertised for job applicants. It filled all its vacancies by word of mouth among existing employees. It saw nepotism as an advantage rather than a drawback and positively encouraged existing employees to spread the word among their relatives when a job vacancy occurred.

Some would argue that this is casting the net too narrowly. However, for a small firm not wishing to go to any great expense to fill a vacancy, spreading the word locally can be an effective means of attracting candidates, particularly at a time of high unemployment.

The word-of-mouth method is, however, very much frowned upon by professional recruiters and the Equal Opportunities Commission. Potentially it could result in indirect discrimination and the company concerned could ultimately find itself brought before an industrial tribunal.

Say, for example, all current employees are white

males. Most of their friends may also be white males, so that is who they will tell of the vacancy. If word of mouth is the only method, ethnic minorities and women are more likely to be excluded, simply because they never get to hear about the job vacancy.

Another limited measure is to advertise the job on the company notice board. There may be highly suitable candidates internally for the job. Equally, existing employees may know of a friend or relative who stands a good chance of fitting the bill.

ADVERTISING

When it comes to media advertising, there are a lot of decisions to be made. Do you advertise in the trade press, the local press or the national press, for example? The answer to these questions will depend largely on the nature of the job and how much you are prepared to spend.

Advertising in the trade press will certainly guarantee that you reach the people in the industry sector in which you operate. It is probably the ideal medium to advertise jobs that are technically-orientated. It is probably better to advertise broader scope jobs in the general press – either locally or nationally. If you are seeking one in the locality of your organization and you don't want to pay the inevitably high costs of advertising nationally, a local newspaper would probably meet your needs.

The advertising department of your chosen newspaper will often help you with the wording and layout, if it is a display advertisement, but the assistance will be very rudimentary. For professional advice you would be better off going to an advertising agency or an executive search and selection consultancy, of which there are an enormous number. This will, however, take you into the big league as far as costs are concerned. Professional agencies charge high fees both for helping to find a shortlist of candidates and for advertising on the appointments pages of high-profile newspapers. (More on that in the next chapter.)

D-I-Y Advertising

If you do decide to do your own advertising there are a number of pitfalls to avoid. Always aim to keep the advertisements simple and to the point. That way you won't blur your message and you will keep the costs down. Too often people try to copy the high-flown language of the major multinationals (which have huge budgets for such advertising) and end up with gobbledy-gook, which is simply a waste of space and money.

First-time advertisers tend not to think through the purpose of the advertisement. They overlook the fact that a good advertisement should aim to screen out unsuitable candidates – as well as attracting the right calibre of applicant. Badly worded recruitment advertisements can lead to an overwhelming response. The recruiter ends up having to wade through hundreds of unsuitable applications. It will only be possible to isolate the appropriate candidates after a laborious screening process.

Some people are never put off, of course, however well the advertisement is worded. People who are desperate for a job – and there are many in today's climate of high unemployment – will always chance their arm, however patently unsuitable they are for the vacancy in question. They are determined to get any sort of employment. Nevertheless, the number of unsuitable applicants will be greatly reduced by a carefully worded advertisement.

Avoid any exaggeration. It is far better to be clear and

honest about what the job entails and not hint that there are untold opportunities to be enjoyed by the successful applicant if this is patently not the case.

Ingredients of the job
The four key elements of a job advertisement are:

- the nature of the company/organization concerned and its location
- what the job entails
- the technical and social competencies required
- the rewards on offer

Not everyone believes in including the salary, but doing so can avoid a lot of extra work. Again, a clearly stated salary figure can screen out people who are unsuitable.

Take, for example, the job of a sales manager. It can cover a very broad spectrum. Simply saying that the salary is negotiable gives little clue as to the level of the person being sought. On the other hand, if the job is advertised for a sales manager at £30K per annum, sales managers already earning £50K a year are not going to waste their time – or yours – applying.

By failing to include the salary you are not only clouding the issue, when the purpose of a job advertisement is to do exactly the opposite. You are also giving the impression that you have something to hide – perhaps that what you are prepared to pay is below the industry norm and you are self-conscious about it.

Enticing
What the skilled recruiter tries to do is entice the group of people who are reasonably successful in their current jobs (apart from graduates and school-leavers) but are beginning to feel a little restless. They may not have

thought of moving until they read the advertisement, but it says enough to make them think that perhaps they ought to be considering the idea. An increase in salary is unlikely to be the critical factor. Most people are looking for a modest 15% to 20% increase. If it is a lot more, they may doubt whether it is a job within their capability.

The advertised salary should be roughly in the expected area. The rest of the text should be telling the reader that this is the kind of company that he or she would find pleasant to work for – conveying the values of the company, its size, organization structure, its trends, and the really interesting parts of the job.

What is the job? If it is for a sales manager, for example, how many sales people will be reporting to him or her and what is the territory to be covered?

Similarly, you should include the essential qualities you are looking for in the person to fill the job. You should concentrate on the qualities that are absolutely essential for performing the job efficiently. You should avoid the qualities that might be desirable, but are not essential – avoid fuzzy qualitative descriptions like 'self-starter', 'energetic' or 'ambitious'. Few people would admit that they were not ambitious or that they needed to be 'cranked up' in the morning.

If you want someone with particular qualifications or a certain experience, say so. Stick to your brief and only consider applicants who have the specific qualities you are after.

The cost of an advertisement can be considerably reduced by putting most of the information into the job description or other material sent to enquirers. There remains, of course, a real risk that an advertisement that contains too little information will fail to attract people of the right calibre.

Discrimination

It is important to avoid anything in the wording of an advertisement that appears to be discriminatory. In some instances, it is illegal to discriminate, but the enlightened recruiter should not solely be guided by whether there are sanctions under the law. The main aim should be to operate in an ethical and fair-minded way. Doing so will not merely protect the recruiting organization from legal recriminations; it will also signal to the world at large the organization's prevailing culture. If an organization recruits ethically, it is most likely to operate ethically.

Discrimination on the grounds of sex, race or religion are fairly obvious. Most magazines and newspapers have staff who will scan advertising copy to avoid any contraventions of the law, if only to protect their own position. Less obvious is discrimination on the grounds of age. This can easily occur unintentionally.

Age discrimination

In the United States age discrimination in job advertisements is illegal and in France it is illegal to set upper age limits on job vacancies. At the moment, older people in Britain are unprotected by the law where job advertisements are concerned.

Although there are sometimes valid reasons for seeking youthful applicants, most sensible recruiters concentrate on fitness for the job and the right experience and background. It is a cliché to say some people are old at 30 and others young at 60, but the amount of energy and dedication people bring to a job hardly ever depends on their age.

In the 1980s there was something of a youth cult in

Britain, but there are signs that employers are again seeking the value of experience. They would be foolish to ignore the large pool of redundant executives who have passed the age of 50, who for reasons outside their control find themselves looking for a job.

Response requirements

Job advertisements should make clear the kind of response expected. Should applicants telephone or write in? Do they have a choice? Will you be sending an application form? If so, don't ask for a CV – you will be asking for the same information twice.

A survey by consultants Price Waterhouse among 200 senior executive job seekers revealed that sending a CV is still the most popular method for 66 per cent of the people questioned, but there has been a considerable increase in the percentage favouring a telephone reply.

A recent innovation for graduate recruiters is telephone screening. After receiving an enquiry, or a completed application form, companies ask undergraduates to telephone them. Specific, targeted questions, related to job competencies, are asked over the telephone. It takes the form of a highly structured interview or a biodata questionnaire (see Chapter 6).

If the student 'passes' this initial phase, he or she qualifies for the next stage – a face-to-face interview or assessment centre. The advantages for the recruiter are obvious. It achieves an interview of sorts without the time and expense of travel. If you are wondering about the poor impecunious student's telephone bill, it should be added that the recruiting organizations normally call the student back once contact is made.

You should make it clear to whom job applicants should apply and at what address. It is quite helpful to include a closing date, so that you don't continue to be flooded with applicants long after you have already arrived at a promising shortlist.

Example
The advertisement prepared by MSL International, a leading search and selection consultancy, for Ealing Hospital NHS Trust (for publication in the Health Service Journal) illustrates well how the essentials of a job can be covered within a small amount of space (Figure 2.1). Readers can see at a glance which organization has the vacancy, what the position is and the remuneration package on offer.

The advertisement then goes on to give succinct details of the working environment. The number of hospital beds, the size of the operating budget and the number of people employed all help to form a picture of the scale of the work.

It is honestly stated that the trust is working in a difficult climate and operating at a deficit, while holding out the prospect of a bright future. This leads naturally into the medium-term challenges the new job-holder will have to tackle – 'eliminating the deficit and improving the range and quality of services'.

Following on logically from that, the advertisement sets out both the technical and interpersonal requirements of the job. Finally, the advertisement names the person to contact for further information and states that applicants should send a CV before a given closing date. It makes a point of saying that it is an equal opportunity employer, serving a multi-ethnic community in West London.

Substance rather than show
The Price Waterhouse survey of 200 senior executive job seekers found that only 2 per cent were attracted by

advertisements featuring pictures or other graphic devices, with 88 per cent saying they preferred plain text. Age may have been a factor since it is generally recognized that younger people may see more adventurous design as a reflection of an interesting corporate culture.

The desire for substance rather than show emerged even more clearly when people were asked for their views on the wording of advertisements. The continual use of words such as 'proactive', 'challenging', 'dynamic', and 'visionary' seems to turn many potential candidates off.

That view is shared by a recruitment consultant who has compiled a personal blacklist of over-used words: 'crisis management' and 'management of change' are high on the list.

GRADUATE RECRUITMENT

Graduate recruitment calls for an entirely different approach. First of all, it is important to recognize two distinct groups. There are *post*graduates who have already gained their degree and are looking for work. In an economic recession, a high proportion of the previous year's graduates are still unemployed, providing a large pool of people anxious to find jobs.

Then there are the *under*graduates who are still at university studying. They are beginning to think about the job they would like to do when they have finished their studies. They can be approached via the careers departments to be found at most universities.

A university careers department is like an internal job centre. It provides information about job vacancies. In addition, it arranges facilities for employers to visit the campus and interview undergraduates. The annual

Chief E

c£60,000

Ealing Hospital is a modern general hospital with 450 beds, providing comprehensive acute care and accident and emergency services for a large multi-ethnic community in West London. The Trust, which has an operating budget of about £40m and employs 1,200 people, is acknowledged as a preferred supplier by the local Health Authorities and although currently operating in a difficult financial climate, has a manageable deficit and a bright future.

The particular challenges facing the new Chief Executive will be to eliminate the deficit, to generate new income, and to develop and communicate the long term strategy for the Trust. Working closely with an able and supportive Board, the Chief Executive will further develop existing centres of excellence and implement new initiatives to improve the

 **MSL** In

CONSULTANTS IN S

EALING
HOSPITAL
NHS TRUST

ecutive

ar + PRP

ınge and quality of services to the local ›mmunity.

You will have held a senior management osition in the Health Service or in an ·ganisation of comparable complexity. Strong ersonal credibility, maturity and leadership ualities will characterise your management yle. Your achievements will demonstrate your ɔility to meet quality, performance and financial ırgets, identify new opportunities and build usinesses.

If you would like further information about this ıteresting and challenging opportunity, please ɔntact Carolyn Ritchie at MSL Group Ltd, 2 Aybrook Street, London W1M 3JL. Tel: 71 487 5000. Fax: 071 465 8957. Please apply by ending a CV, quoting reference. H5592 before)th December 1993.

The Trust is an equal opportunity employer.

rnational

:H AND SELECTION

CLIENT APPROVAL

CLEARANCE DEADLINE:

SIGNATURE:

DATE:

Fig. 2.1 *Example of a succinct job advertisement that packs in a lot of information*

round of visits by the big employers to the main universities throughout the country has become something of a major jamboree and is known as the 'Milk Round'.

In the boom days of the mid-1980s the Milk Round was highly competitive. Today, with so much unemployment, it is a buyer's market, but high-flyers are still a scarce resource and employers go to some considerable lengths to attract graduates. The major employers, such as the leading multinational companies and the big accountancy groups, produce expensive four-colour brochures extolling the virtues of working for their particular organization.

Videos and novels
Some companies produce videos for graduates to watch at their leisure. One enterprising accountancy firm – KPMG Peat Marwick – once even went to the trouble to produce a spoof Mills & Boon type romantic paperback, featuring an accountant as the key character.

Graduates who demonstrate high potential will be invited back for further interviews and sometimes entertained at wine and cheese evenings.

The Milk Round is a very specialized area of recruitment. It has spawned an industry of its own. The Association of Graduate Recruiters acts as a best practice information source and liaison centre. Some large companies, particularly the big accountancy groups who recruit hundreds of graduates a year, employ fulltime executives who do nothing else but run a graduate recruitment office. Clearly, if you are a small organization planning to recruit graduates, the most obvious advice is that the Milk Round isn't something to be entered upon lightly, given the big league competition you are up against.

Concentration

The Milk Round has its good points and one of them is that it concentrates the recruitment activity. It runs from December to March, but most of the interviews are conducted in February. Accountancy firms, which like to steal a march on rival recruiters, usually run their Milk Rounds in December at the end of the autumn term or semester.

If the Milk Round were not so highly focused students could well find themselves spending most of their final year at university applying for jobs. Application forms can take several hours to complete and since a student is likely to apply to as many as ten organizations, it involves a heavy commitment of time.

The Milk Round is an attempt to distil that into a concentrated period at the end of the autumn. Students are then left to concentrate on their final exams.

Work experience

The Milk Round is a hugely expensive operation for companies to mount. They have to put together a team of staff to visit maybe 40 universities throughout the country. Some companies find it too much of a circus and have reduced the number of universities they visit annually. Sainsbury's, for example, which recruits around 100 graduates a year as management trainees, now targets specific universities with which it has ongoing relationships – mainly those it co-operates with in designing and funding courses.

In addition, the retail group invites graduates to spend a day working in one of its stores during vacation time to experience the retail environment first-hand. This also gives store staff the opportunity to evaluate the suitability of the graduates for retail work.

Most of the graduates invited take up the offer. This has

greatly helped to reduce the company's staff turnover rate. A high proportion of the people leaving the company do so within the first six months.

KEY POINTS

- Do-it-yourself recruitment or professional advice?
- Pick the right media for your advertisement
- Keep advertisements simple and to the point
- Well-worded advertisements screen out as well as attract
- Avoid judgemental words in advertisements
- Advertisements should be accurate and honest
- Watch out for discrimination
- Graduates can be approached through university career departments
- The Milk Round is a highly competitive and expensive exercise
- Company brochures and videos aimed at graduates can help in recruitment
- Work experience programmes help filter out the graduates who are serious about seeking a job at your organization.

3

PROFESSIONAL ADVICE

When seeking professional advice on how to attract job applicants, there is a hierarchy of agencies which roughly corresponds with the corporate pyramid. At the base are the high street job agencies, such as Manpower and Alfred Marks or lesser known local agencies, which have databases of people looking for jobs mainly at the lower end of the market. You simply tell them your requirements. If they don't already have someone suitable on their database they will stick a card in the window. If they find you the candidate you are after they will charge you a fee, normally based on a proportion of the first year's salary.

For middle and senior management jobs, recruiters normally turn to executive selection consultants and executive search experts (otherwise known as headhunters).

EXECUTIVE SELECTION
Executive selection specialists will take over the responsibility for the time-consuming process of attracting the candidates and arriving at a shortlist. Their services normally include:

- preparing a brief
- advice on the most appropriate media in which to advertise
- designing and writing the advertisement
- carrying out the initial interviews
- drawing up a shortlist

Selection specialists sometimes make use of external databases. They may have a small in-house database, but this will most likely be comprised primarily of people they have identified as prospective candidates for previous job vacancies who did not get past the shortlist stage. This is often supplemented by job seekers who write in 'cold', enquiring whether there are any vacancies on the books.

There are a host of executive selection consultancies. PA Consulting Group, MSL and Hoggett Bowers are among the better known ones.

There are some obvious reasons why organizations prefer to advertise through the anonymity of intermediaries. Sometimes it is because the incumbent in the job is not performing to requirements but the organization concerned wants to keep it secret that it is seeking a replacement. There may also be a reason for keeping the advertised salary anonymous – perhaps because it is higher than normal and the recruiting organization wishes to avoid sowing seeds of discontent among its existing staff.

In both these cases, the job can be advertised under the logo of the selection consultancy and nobody will be any the wiser until a decision has been taken.

The services selection consultants provide are, however, usually much broader than simply placing an advertisement. They can also help the client organization to draw up a specification for the job, which will include:

- an understanding of the organization
- the content of the job
- why the job is available
- the reporting structures involved
- the accountability
- the candidate profile

Steering clients away from the pitfalls
Sometimes the selection consultancy will advise clients to seek candidates quite different from those they first

had in mind. If it is a replacement job, clients will quite often be looking for someone similar to the previous incumbent. Nevertheless, times change and the requirements of the job change too. Often new factors need to be taken into account.

The client is sometimes unaware of the prevailing forces in the recruitment market and as a result sets out to seek the impossible. One company, for example, was advised that the job it intended to advertise could be performed partly in-house by an existing executive and partly by outsourcing. It was pointed out to the client that the candidate it was seeking did not exist at the salary it was prepared to pay.

Selection consultants often advise clients on the outputs they should be seeking in a new executive recruit. This is particularly helpful in the case of non-executive directors who find themselves on the board of an organization in an industrial sector of which they may not have any technical experience.

Selection specialists, because they are more objective, can help to find candidates who are compatible with an organization's culture. They are usually more realistic in recommending who will fit into an organization's prevailing environment.

Fees
The fees of selection consultants, not surprisingly, are higher than those charged by the high street employment agencies. They will normally charge between 18 and 24 per cent of the first year's salary. Essentially what they are offering is to free the recruiter of all the hard slog of arriving at a shortlist. The recruiter is presented with perhaps five or six people from which to make a choice without all the rigmarole of having to wade through dozens of application forms.

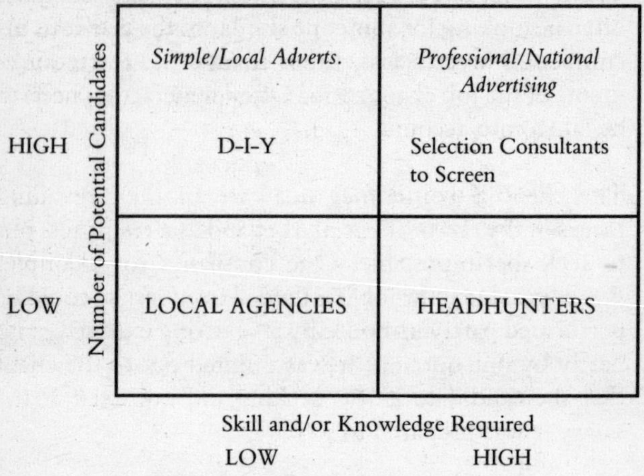

	Simple/Local Adverts. D-I-Y	Professional/National Advertising Selection Consultants to Screen
HIGH		
LOW	LOCAL AGENCIES	HEADHUNTERS

Number of Potential Candidates (left axis label)

Skill and/or Knowledge Required
LOW   HIGH

Fig. 3.1   *Comparative use of Local Agencies, Selection Consultants and Headhunters*

Also, bear in mind that reputable professional recruitment agencies are experienced at what they do and, in theory at least, should be better at it. Reason dictates that they are more likely to arrive at an objective shortlist than an organization that is only recruiting on an irregular basis.

HEADHUNTERS
At the top end of the market are the executive search consultants or headhunters. They rarely advertise.

The distinctive factor when choosing between search and selection through an advertisement is the size of the pool of people who could possibly do the job. The smaller the choice, the more headhunting becomes the most viable option. There is, after all, no certainty an advertisement will be read by the small number of people suitable.

The scarcity of potential candidates often correlates

with higher paid jobs, but it can also relate to highly skilled specialists whose talents are scarce. The pool of potential candidates can be equally small, suggesting that headhunting is the most appropriate method.

It is not difficult to identify the companies in which these scarce specialists work. The difficult part is actually finding out their names and enticing them to consider working for another organization. Headhunting is a much better way of attempting to do that than advertising because there is only a very limited number of people involved – often fewer than 200.

Art or science?

Headhunters normally track down their quarry by detective work, which has imbued them with something of a 'cloak and dagger' image. In the past headhunters have tended to enjoy this air of mystique which created the impression that their skills were based on art rather than science. Today, most headhunters stress that their work is very much a structured process more closely akin to science.

Most headhunters will tell you that it is simply hard graft and a certain amount of Sherlock Holmes deduction that helps them to eke out senior level executives who may well be thin on the ground.

One leading headhunter, who only takes on assignments involving annual salaries of £70,000 plus, has a simple formula for finding the perfect candidate. He turns the job inside out. If he is seeking a marketing director, he talks to senior buyers and asks them to nominate the best in the field. Vice-versa, if he is seeking a buying director, he talks to marketing directors to obtain their views of the best available talent.

Adopting this simple but effective ploy, he tracked

down a property director for a leading retail group by contacting estate agents who sell out-of-town sites. One property director's name cropped up repeatedly among the recommendations. The headhunter, who prides himself on the speed with which he fills top level vacancies, had to look no further. He had saved himself the burdensome task of wading through lengthy lists of potential candidates.

Rifle shot

Comparing headhunting to advertised selection is the difference between a rifle shot and a scatter gun approach. A telephone call from an executive search consultant to a potential candidate provides the opportunity to sell the job on offer. The headhunter has much more scope than an advertisement to be very persuasive and present the job in an attractive light.

Search consultants like MSL have networks of 'informers' throughout the UK and Europe who help them track down potential candidates. These informers are often specialists in particular industrial sectors. Many of them are executives who have themselves been head-hunted previously and have become part of a self-perpetuating system.

The price of expertise

Headhunters' expertise does not come cheap. They can charge anything up to 36 per cent of the first year's salary of the successful candidate. This is usually divided into three separate payments – a third on taking up the assignment, a third on providing the shortlist and the final third when the selected individual commences at the client firm.

Considering that most headhunters will only take on jobs worth £50K and above the costs can be pretty high. Occasionally they will work for a fixed rate. The construction industry, for example, has a tradition of using headhunters on this basis.

If it is decided to place an advertisement, that will be added to the cost. Display advertisements in national newspapers are also expensive. Headhunters argue, of course, that their charges are a small price to pay for finding a top executive who can make all the difference to an organization's success or failure. They can all recite graphic accounts of how a company's share price rose dramatically after the installation of a headhunted chief executive.

Some consultancies combine selection and headhunting, but the two activities are usually run as two separate operations. There are search and selection organizations such as the PSD Group that have specialist divisions devoted to particular sectors of the recruitment market (i.e. legal, property, insurance and electronics).

Ethics

Although there are a number of very reputable executive search firms, headhunting is still trying to live down criticisms that have been levelled at it over the years. A survey of personnel directors and top executives from 200 medium-sized UK companies revealed that 25 per cent regarded headhunters as outright cowboys, 33 per cent saw them as inexperienced, 45 per cent felt they were arrogant and 54 per cent thought they were overpaid.

Complaints varied between unprofessional or unethical behaviour and sloppy research. Nearly half of all the respondents said they had personal experience of consultants recommending candidates to them without initial screening. A quarter had also experienced consultants poaching staff from among their own client companies. Equally worrying, according to the survey, was that 44 per cent had received names and CVs from headhunters without the candidates concerned having been notified beforehand.

This disquiet about the conduct of some headhunters could account for the rapid turnover among consultants used by companies. The survey showed that 22 per cent of companies use more than four different recruitment consultants a year, a level of loyalty that is low compared to other service professionals.

Proof of the pudding

There are rogue elements in all professions. It is fair to say that the majority of executive search consultants undoubtedly carry out an important function and satisfied clients return to them time and time again to benefit from their professionalism. The proof of the pudding of course is in the eating. If they find the right people and take over all the hard work involved, clients will return for more of the same service.

There are other objective measures: how long new recruits stay with the organization that recruits them; how they get on with their colleagues; whether they strike up a rapport with customers, improve business results and earn their keep, to name but a few.

The problem is that these objective indicators are rarely measured. The fee is charged, the work completed and the search consultant moves on to the next assignment. Headhunters don't get the full fee until the job candidate has been appointed. They receive the same amount however long it takes to find a suitable applicant. There is considerable pressure on them to come up with a quick solution, rather than taking the time to do an extensive trawl which might net an even better candidate.

Because measurement can only be made long after the applicant is hired, there is no immediate feedback loop to establish whether the chosen candidate has in fact fulfilled the requirements of the job.

COST

From the cost point of view, there is not a great deal to choose between headhunting and advertised selection.

PA charges a third of the first year's salary for executive search. The charge for using a selection consultant is between 20 per cent and 25 per cent of the first year's salary. But when you add to that the cost of a display advertisement on the Appointments Page of a national newspaper, there are few – if any – savings.

KEY POINTS

- Professional advisers come in three main forms:
  - high street job agencies
  - executive selection consultants
  - executive search consultants (headhunters)
- Professional advisers can provide anonymity and reduce the workload
- Selection specialists short-circuit the process by presenting clients with a shortlist
- Headhunters fish in a small pool and can target more effectively
- Some 'cowboy' consultancies give headhunting a bad name.

4

SCREENING THE APPLICANTS

If you have worded your advertisement well you should not be bombarded by an avalanche of irrelevant responses and sorting the wheat from the chaff should not be too onerous. A lot of organizations send application forms to job applicants. These can be useful for whittling down the number of people who seem worth interviewing. Other organizations only use CVs, especially where higher level jobs are concerned.

APPLICATION FORMS

In favour of application forms

The advantage of an application form is that you control the information you obtain from the candidates. You can then screen them all against the same criteria and not against handwriting or grammar or how they happen to put their CV together. You can cover ground that may not be included in the average CV, such as ethnic origin.

The Equal Opportunities Commission expects companies to monitor the sex and race composition of job applicants as well as employees, so that the company can be confident it is not discriminating unfairly. There have been some celebrated cases appearing before industrial tribunals where applicants have alleged discrimination. The tribunal has taken a very dim view if an employer has not taken steps to monitor sex and race of applicants so as to be able to provide evidence to the tribunal that it has fair recruitment practices.

Another argument in favour of application forms is that they can help to indicate the intentions of the applicant. If job applicants are serious they will take the time to fill out the application form. Casual applicants won't bother. The recruiter has no need to waste valuable time on the latter.

Against application forms

There are some cogent arguments against the application form. For example, senior managers and professionals are put off by them. In this case, there are usually few applicants and the people involved tend to be incredibly busy. Asking for a CV is probably quite adequate in these circumstances. It basically comes down to selection ratios – i.e. the ratio of applicants to the jobs available.

Ian Duff, writing in an August 1993 issue of *The Sunday Times* suggests that application forms blunt the initiative of the applicant. They elicit the same information as can be found on the CV but often include additional questions such as: 'Describe yourself in one hundred words'; or 'What are your greatest achievements and failures?'

Duff argues that the CV is a better tool. It is a chance for applicants to sell themselves. Its presentation and its content are also more useful and less boring to the member of staff who has to do the scrutinizing.

Some recruiters ask applicants to send a covering letter with their CV or application form setting out why they think their experience is relevant to the job. This can also be quite effective in screening out half-hearted applications. Some applicants ignore the request and simply send their CV, which raises questions about their ability to follow instructions or their enthusiasm for getting the job. Some who do send the requested covering letter are so lengthy or imprecise that it raises worries about their ability to communicate concisely – a key generic skill.

ARRIVING AT A SHORTLIST

If your advertisement or job brief has skilfully covered
the job specification, most of your applicants should be
of the calibre you are looking for, although you will
always get one or two mavericks who will try for any
job going regardless of how inappropriate their experience. You should use the same job specification to
screen the applications to arrive at a shortlist.

There is a very simple technique for drawing up a shortlist. Take a sheet of paper and draw two columns on it.
In the lefthand column write 'definite candidates'. In the
righthand column write 'possible candidates'. Stick to
that rigidly.

There is a strong temptation to deviate from this simple
screening process. An application comes in and there is
something in it you hadn't thought about previously.
You feel compelled to see the person concerned and you
ignore the fact that this applicant lacks some of the qualities that qualify him or her for your 'definites' or 'possibles' column. While a recruiter should always keep an
open mind, you should think very hard before you
break your own rules. The best policy is probably to reject all those who don't correspond with your original
criteria. Otherwise, why go to so much trouble to draw
up the job specification in the first place?

If it turns out that you have an insufficient number of
'definites' among your applicants, take another look at
the candidates you have relegated to the 'possibles' category. Reconsider if any of them can be upgraded to
your priority list. If not, you would probably be best
advised to re-advertise the job vacancy, perhaps via a
different medium. If you have an adequate number of
'definites', pick the ten to 15 most promising candidates
in order of priority and that gives you your interview
list.

If you have 50 applicants and you are only prepared to

interview 15, invite the first 15 in order of priority. You may keep another five or six in reserve as a backstop in case all the applicants on your priority list turn out to be disappointing on interview. Discard the rest of the applications. There is no point in holding on to them unless you want to keep a file for future reference.

Rejection

Some organizations are very discourteous when it comes to turning applicants down. Some don't even acknowledge receipt of the application, which is just sheer bad manners. There are even heartless recruiters who consign no-hope applications to the waste bin without a second thought. They give applicants the same amount of attention as leaflets advertising life insurance and time shares.

Such callous treatment is contemptible. Applicants should always know where they stand. They should be informed that their application has been received and roughly how long it is likely to take to consider it. If you can see at a glance that applicants are unsuitable, turn them down quickly. There is nothing to be gained from keeping them in suspense. It only creates an impression of an uncaring and thoughtless organization. Some of the applicants may be your customers.

Negative option letter

In the current state of the job market 90 per cent of applicants will often not even get the satisfaction of a job interview. Rejection may well breed resentment towards the recruiting company.

In an article from an August 1993 issue of *The Times*, Peter French (MD of Select Security Recruitment Ltd) observed that an insensitive rejection letter may well sabotage the efforts of the company's marketing department. The increasing use of the negative option letter – one which imposes a time limit stating that the application has failed if the company has not contacted the applicant by a set date – is becoming an easy way out for personnel departments overwhelmed by the response to a particular recruitment advertisement.

When subjected to this impersonal approach, writes French, the applicant tends to feel resentment against the recruiter's apparent indifference.

A stereotype letter of rejection is perfectly acceptable. Nobody expects an organization dealing with a large number of applicants to write personal letters of response. All you need to do is thank the unsuccessful applicants for their trouble, but explain that you have received a lot of applications (if this is true) and that there are other people more appropriately qualified and experienced.

Rejection letters should be signed by the decision maker. It is insulting to send a rejection letter *per pro* or with a computer generated signature.

If for some reason you are going to have to sit on the applications for a couple of weeks, try to write and let applicants know. However, generally speaking, once you have received the bulk of the applications you should get on with the screening process as quickly as possible. The best applicants won't hang around for ever. They may have more than one job opportunity in their portfolio. The desperate job seekers will be patient but they are almost certainly not the applicants you are after.

Losing the good applicants
The good applicants probably have sufficient confidence in their job seeking abilities to back out if you

treat them badly. That may mean you lose all the good candidates and retain the mediocre ones.

This may sound like an obvious point. But like so much common sense, it isn't commonly applied. One well-known employer was recruiting a director to set up an operation in France. The job specification was extremely challenging and the candidate specification a tough one to match.

Advertisements were placed throughout the UK and continental Europe. It was decided that all the short-listed candidates should meet the company's existing directors – a very protracted procedure when the trawl is throughout an entire continent. The upshot was that the best candidate became tired of waiting for his rival applicants to be seen. When he was finally offered the job he had long since accepted an alternative position.

The person ultimately appointed to the job was less than satisfactory and the company closed its French operation after two years with a loss of £1 million on the venture. This just goes to show that even blue chip companies that ought to know better are capable of making fundamental mistakes.

REFERENCES
Much of the effort that goes into reference checking is misplaced, according to Nick and Rowena Cowan, two experts in personnel management. Writing in the December 1989 issue of *Personnel Management* magazine, they suggest that the vast majority of references add nothing to the quality of the selection decision. Yet, they contend, properly and competently carried out, reference checking is an essential part of the recruitment process.

References are essentially a way of double-checking

whether what the job applicant has told you about his or her experience or qualifications is in fact true. It is far easier to check facts than it is to check character. Since interpersonal skills are increasingly important in modern organizations this presents something of a problem.

You can easily find out if the educational or professional qualifications a candidate claims to possess stand up to scrutiny. Most educational establishments and professional institutions keep records which will verify or otherwise what the applicant has told you. It is surprising how few recruiters take the time to carry out this basic safeguard. There are many horror stories of people joining organizations with fake qualifications which lead to situations of embarrassment for everyone concerned.

To cite an actual example, a candidate gave as a referee a senior figure at an overseas hospital where he had previously worked. The recruiter duly wrote. A few weeks later two references arrived, both on headed notepaper from the hospital and both purportedly signed by the doctor given as a referee. One letter said it was impossible to make any comment since the doctor didn't know the job applicant. The other letter gave a glowing reference. Unsurprisingly, further investigation revealed the glowing reference to be a fake.

When it comes to checking character references, the recruiter is on even less certain ground, because the names of the referees are almost always supplied by the job applicant. Candidates are highly unlikely to select a referee who will speak badly of them. There are two kinds of references in this category:

- personal references
- job references

Personal references

These are people who are supposed to know the applicant well on a personal basis. They can be anyone from the local vicar to a personal friend. Some organizations specify that it should not be a relative. But it is highly questionable whether there is anything to be gained from following these up. If applicants cannot find two people in the world who will say something good about them they must be social outcasts!

Occasionally, personal referees will let slip something about the candidate that sets off alarm bells. Maybe a hint that the person concerned is over-indulgent where drink is concerned or that if roused he or she has a rather nasty temper. However, it is unlikely that personal referees will overtly reveal shortcomings about a close acquaintance, especially as they are fully aware that an offguard comment might jeopardize the job opportunity.

Job references

Job references are probably more relevant, but again you have to ask yourself what you will gain from contacting a previous employer. Even if the previous employers are glad to see the back of a candidate, it is unlikely they will reveal anything of great significance. The only valid employment referees are individuals with first-hand detailed knowledge of a candidate's work.

The practice of asking for one or two referees who are friends and colleagues is, generally, a waste of time. In the first place, candidates are hardly likely to nominate someone who they suspect will provide a poor reference. Secondly, such referees are rarely likely to be knowledgeable about the individual's current work performance. Thirdly, you can never be sure how much careful thought will be given in replying to the query and, finally, you have no means of assessing the referee's knowledge or judgement.

In checking any reference, the prime aim should be to double check factual information. It is important to ascertain that a particular candidate worked at such-and-such a firm for a certain period of time, especially if you are looking for someone with that kind of experience. For example, if you are seeking an experienced sales manager who has spent at least five years with a leading firm in a similar product area, it is vital to confirm that this was the case with a previous employer.

The art of exaggeration

It might also be prudent to check that the experience was of the nature you are seeking. Some candidates are expert at exaggerating their CVs and making unexceptional jobs look important. One of the authors (Shackleton) was recently asked to help a company recruit a marketing assistant. A requirement was that candidates, mostly recent graduates, should be able to use spreadsheets. The shortlist of six, all of whom claimed to be familiar with spreadsheets, were invited for tests and interviews.

During the day candidates were asked if they would mind doing a straightforward spreadsheet exercise on a personal computer. At this point one candidate admitted that she knew nothing about computers and another that he could only use word processors. Of the remaining four, one clearly had only the faintest idea of how to work the spreadsheets and just three of the original six lived up to their claims of expertise.

Interviewing the referee

Effective reference checking is of prime importance in the case of managerial appointments – or any appointment where the ability to achieve results is essential. Recruitment experts suggest that the starting point should be with the candidate's line boss in previous relevant positions and in the current job. This entails talking to referees directly by telephone or, on occasion, face-to-face.

It calls for skilled interviewing techniques – asking the right questions, pressing to get the key issues, evaluating the responses and judging the value of what is said. The interviewer has to discern the truth, particularly when differences in key matters are revealed between what the candidate has said and what the referee says.

Competency-based references
To avoid vague answers from referees you should ask specific questions. An obvious one is: Would you employ this person again? Equally: Why did this person leave you? Better still, base your questions on the competencies required for the job. This means asking about specific incidents and events in the candidate's career. You should ask the employer, for example, what was the last major project the candidate was involved in and how well he or she carried it out.

Assuming the employer answers truthfully, this will give you specific insight into how good the candidate is at assessing difficulties, planning for obstacles, controlling time and resources and many other qualities associated with undertaking a major project.

When seeking a reference over the telephone, hesitation, and the careful choice of words can indicate deception or an unwillingness to be truthful on the part of the referee.

Written versus verbal references
People are reluctant to give written references, because they are worried about libel. In fact, they need not be concerned. Unless it can be proven that malice was intended, an accusation of libel or slander in relation to a

job reference will not stand up in court. But many people are unaware of where the law draws the line and they prefer to play safe.

Referees feel a lot safer giving an opinion about a former employee over the telephone than committing their views to paper, which could be used in evidence against them. It is also a lot easier answering a quick telephone inquiry than having to compose a reference, which is likely to be pretty bland anyway.

Written references have the distinct drawback of not permitting discussion, a prime requisite of effective reference checking in the opinion of many experts. Nick and Rowena Cowan warn against the 'neutral' written reference that purposely avoids any negative comment. The authors refer to a number of standard signals that should alert recruiters to the fact that the referee is striving more to be diplomatic than factual. Such references are bland and unhelpful:

'Mr Jones was employed by this company from February 14th 1988 to September 16th 1990 and carried out his duties as a sales manager to my satisfaction during that time. He met the requirements of the job and was generally liked by his colleagues. We wish him well in his future work.'

No mention of the candidate's achievements or contribution to his previous employment. Nothing negative, but nothing particularly positive either. Damning by faint praise is usually obvious, but recruiters should also be alert to damning by omission. A reference for someone responsible for the management of cash which did not mention honesty or trustworthiness would obviously sound alarm bells.

Experts counsel that all references should be read in a

questioning frame of mind. Why is a particular feature mentioned? Does 'a social and gregarious individual' possibly mean 'he likes to drink a bit too much'?

Recruiters would be wise to follow up any such signals. Although the referee might be reluctant to be more explicit on paper, he or she may well be prepared to go into greater detail over the telephone.

KEY POINTS

- Application forms:
  - enable candidates to be screened against the same criteria (positive)
  - can cover ethnic origin and identify the more serious candidates (positive)
  - can blunt initiative (negative)
- Divide candidates into 'definites' and 'possibles' to arrive at a shortlist
- Keep applicants informed and always send a rejection letter
- Don't keep candidates waiting for ever
- Don't put too much faith in references
- Consider the telephone reference rather than the written one
- Ask specific questions of referees to avoid vague answers
- Make those questions job and competency specific.

5

THE INTERVIEW

The face-to-face interview is by far the most popular method of assessing job candidates. Yet research shows that the typical, unstructured interview is a poor way to predict which candidate is best suited to the job. It is little better than random choice – you might just as well pick the names out of a hat. Despite such evidence, recruiters persist in making it their favourite method. Most managers believe they are good at interviewing and that interviews are useful selection tools.

Interviews can be a valuable way to get a 'feel' for whether a job applicant is likely to fit in well in your organization. Managers tend to place a lot of faith in such imponderables as 'gut' feel, intuition and personal chemistry. An interview is a good opportunity to test out all such feelings, but taken in isolation it is a dangerous device to rely on. It should really be viewed as just one tool in a recruiter's armoury. It should be combined with a number of more objective and scientifically validated assessment methods outlined in the next chapter.

GOOD AND BAD INTERVIEWING

The interview is definitely here to stay. And there is a big difference between good interviewing and indifferent interviewing. Neil Anderson and Viv Shackleton point out in their book, *Successful Selection Interviewing*, that in their enthusiasm for more modern methods, such as psychometric tests, professional recruiters and researchers tend to look down on interviewing as being merely a less reliable method of essentially the same kind.

The authors argue that while this may be true in the case of bad interviewing, it is not true of skilful interviewing. Good interviewers can tease out the reasons behind successes and failures at work. What's more, they can influence an outstanding candidate into joining their company instead of going to work somewhere else.

The pitfalls

The value of interviewing will be enhanced if the numerous pitfalls that many recruiters fall into are avoided. These traps for the unwary are epitomized by a number of typical interviewing styles:

1. *The Waffler*. A common fault is for the interviewer to spend the whole session rambling on about the organization the candidate may or may not be joining as a result of the application. The candidate learns a lot of vague information about the organization but the interviewer learns very little about the candidate.

2. *The Psycho-Analyst*. At one time there was a fashion for non-directive interviewing. This is virtually the opposite to the waffling style. The interviewer sits impassively like a stuffed turkey hardly uttering a word after inviting candidates to talk about themselves. The interviewer rarely interjects and effectively hands over control of the session to the applicant. This is supposed – like psycho-analysis – to reveal something deeply significant. Experienced interviewers rightly dismiss this approach to selecting and interviewing as being totally ineffective.

3. *The Historian*. There is nothing more tedious than basing the entire interview on the candidate's CV. This interviewer religiously sticks to the candidate's past history, covering every last detail, from birth to current job. This approach certainly covers a lot of ground, but is it likely to glean much information that will help the recruiter to make a rational judgement about the person's suitability for the job? Without probing, asking open questions

or asking how and why (as opposed to what and when), the answer is almost certainly 'no'.

4. *The Aggressor*. This interviewer falsely believes that the only way to get to the real heart of the matter is to make the job applicant as uncomfortable as possible. The Aggressor behaves like an irritated TV interviewer trying to persuade a politician to depart from the party line. Such interviewers harp back to the days when stress interviews were in vogue. They believe in setting stressful traps for their unsuspecting applicants, such as leaving them alone in the interviewing room for an extended period of time. They might even spring nerve-racking surprises, such as asking the job applicant to recite the alphabet backwards.

Thankfully, such extreme methods have been totally discredited. Since stress is only a small part of most jobs, the technique reveals little about how the candidate will handle the more routine aspects of the work. Even when stress is a large part of the job, a so-called stress interview will tell you very little about how candidates will respond to the very different and more job-related stress of, say, presentations, time deadlines, travel, lazy colleagues or constant change. It is also questionable whether stress interviews were ever ethical or fair.

The perfect interview

The Perfect Interviewer eschews all the above pitfalls and is a very different character to those described:

5. *The Fact Finder*. This interviewer will have done a lot of preparation. A decision will have been taken well in advance about what the key aspects of the job are and the questioning will concentrate on those areas. Unlike the Waffler, the Fact Finder will focus on the job analysis and the competencies that have already been pinpointed. This will avoid,

among other things, the interview becoming a cosy fireside chat. It will instead be a purposeful discussion at the end of which both the interviewer and the candidate should have a clear idea of what is on offer.

For example, if you are looking for competence in a skill that is essential for the job, you will need to know what evidence you will accept that the candidate possesses that skill. You will need to be clear in your own mind what you are looking for. The interview is the process by which you establish whether the candidate has this essential skill. You probe for it. If by the end of the session, it is clear that candidates do not have this skill you should reject them. You either find it or you don't.

Probing should involve the use of open questions, followed at a later stage by more closed-ended ones. It's like a funnel:

It starts with broad open questions, such as:
Tell me about your previous job.
What were the difficulties?
How did you cope with them?
What do you see as the challenges of the post you have applied for?
How will you deal with them?

Moving through more specific job-related questions such as:
What experience have you got with local area networks?
What do you know of the latest techniques of electro-plating?
How do you intend to cope with the travel demands?

To closed-ended type questions, such as: What salary are you on?
Do you have a company car?
When can you start?
(Or: Don't ring us, we'll ring you)

CANDIDATES TO GUARD AGAINST

However well prepared the interviewer is, there is, of course, no guarantee that the candidates on the shortlist will turn out to have the ideal qualities being sought. Although they look good on paper, they may well spring some surprises on the interviewer. Here are some typical candidates the vigilant interviewer should guard against:

1. *The Dandy*. This candidate is all show and no substance. He will inevitably be immaculately turned out. But when you try to get down to brass tacks there is something missing. The Dandy will try to gloss over glaring holes in his CV. He will have an excuse for everything and he will not be short of hard luck stories to explain why he does not have the required documents to vouch for his qualifications or why he only lasted a few months in his last three jobs. A short way into the interview you will be wondering if you can believe anything he tells you. Americans call this person 'the empty suit'.

2. *The Know-all*. This candidate is very articulate and self-assured, but she comes across as over-bearing and tends to make outrageous statements about her previous boss. She is very self-opinionated and does not seem to have any time for people with a different point of view. Her career record seems to lack any experience of working with teams or project groups. Is that because her abrasive manner prevents her from co-operating well with others? If her work skills are outstanding you might give her some consideration, but in the age of empowerment and team-building you will probably think twice about allowing this character to stir up a hornets' nest in your organization.

3. *The Frightened Mouse*. This applicant is clearly nervous and is unable to project himself. But when you

probe his skills and experience he seems to have all the right qualifications. What you have to decide is whether it is simply the stress of the interview that makes him so diffident or whether it is a fundamental personality trait. If the latter, you have to decide to what extent that might undermine his effectiveness in the job, referring to the job specification.

4. *The Misfit*. This candidate is keen to tell you about all her achievements, but few seem to relate to the job on offer. When this is pointed out, the Misfit insists that she is very flexible and adaptable. You will be amazed how quickly she manages to pick things up, she assures you. There is nothing that overawes her. This candidate's determination is to be admired, but why take the chance when you have several other candidates with the skills that meet the brief? You should also ask yourself how this person slipped through your initial screening process and managed to get on to the interviewing shortlist. Maybe there is something to be said for her persistence after all.

THE DOS AND DON'TS OF INTERVIEWING
There are a number of useful tips on how to get the best out of interviews.

Draw up a plan of campaign
Make up your mind what you really need to know about the job applicants that is going to tell you that they are suitable for the job on offer. It would probably help to draw up a list of key elements of the job and tick them off during the course of the interview. You don't necessarily have to stick to them in rigid order, but before you call an end to the interview, just check that you have covered all the points you need to know. This will ensure thoroughness and that each candidate is being judged on the same basis.

Avoid interruptions

Make sure you give the candidate your undivided attention. Interruptions from telephone calls or unscheduled
visitors, however urgent they may seem, will disturb
the flow of the interview. This can be very disconcert-
ing for the candidate and will spoil your concentration
as well. Tell your secretary to hold all calls and guard
your door against all-comers.

Put the candidate at ease

To obtain the best impression of candidates help them
to relax. You should be courteous although firm in
your intentions – to arrive at a dispassionate and objective assessment of their skills and aptitudes. You should
at the outset tell the candidate what you are trying to do.
You should explain that there are certain areas of the
candidate's CV that you wish to explore and that there
are certain requirements of the job that you need to
probe to find out if the candidate has the necessary qualities. This makes it plain to the candidate from the start
the kind of interviewer you are and it helps to diffuse
any natural tension.

Some organizations send a written brief of the job
specification to candidates in advance. This avoids
wasting time at the interview going over a lot of dry information and statistics. It is probably a good idea to
start the session off by asking candidates if they have
any questions about the job brief. This is a good
warm-up device to help candidates relax. It puts them
in the driving seat. They can put you on the spot for a
while. What do you mean by this? How have sales
gone? Why did the company make a loss last year?

Alternatively, an easy-to-answer, broad question, such
as 'What does your current job at Smith & Jones involve?', may help to relax a candidate early on. After
that, you, the interviewer, can take control of the

questioning just as the candidate's self-confidence is beginning to grow.

Be aware of body language

Even for the most experienced job seeker interviews are a testing time. You can help candidates to relax by using the right body language. Be cheerful and fulsome in your welcome when candidates arrive. Ask them if they would like any refreshment. Invite them to sit down in a place that does not over-emphasize your commanding position. If possible, it is better to relax on equal terms around a coffee table rather than place the candidate on the opposite side of your working desk.

Watch out too for the candidate's body language. If he or she appears to be sitting uncomfortably in a defensive manner, try to lighten the proceedings with a friendly comment to reduce any tension.

Don't rush

You may be under pressure to process as many applicants as you can in the course of a day, but never short-change a candidate by curtailing the interview. Give all the candidates enough time to present their attributes and give yourself enough time to make a fair assessment. You will be tempted to curtail interviews with candidates you don't instantly take to, but often candidates who take time to warm up turn out to have hidden qualities that are not immediately apparent. If you usher them out of the door too soon you may never know what a boon they could have been to your organization.

Make notes

However much you pride yourself on your memory or your ability to juggle a lot of facts in your head, take the trouble to make brief written notes about each candidate. Seeing one candidate after another is a gruelling exercise and it is very easy to confuse one person's comments with another. You could end up selecting the wrong candidate simply because your recollections of how the interview progressed are incorrect. That is neither fair to the candidates nor beneficial for the organization you represent.

Let the candidate do the talking

The object of the exercise is to get candidates to tell you as much about themselves as time allows. If you indulge in long explanations about what the job entails, candidates will have little opportunity to explain the attributes that they think will set them apart. You will have plenty of time to go into detail about the job once you have made your selection. First, you need to know if the candidate has what it takes to fill the vacancy.

By asking open questions you will help to draw the candidate out and obtain more expansive answers. This is particularly important where nervous candidates are concerned and those who are not naturally articulate. To some extent the quality of their answers will depend on the skill of your questions. You can ask more closed-ended questions to obtain hard facts once you have arrived at an overall impression of the candidate.

Avoid prejudice

We are all inclined to warm to people who share our own interests – or even our own appearance. Conversely, we tend to resist those types who are unsympathetic to our own likes and dislikes. Don't allow bias to creep into your judgement. Although you may have to consider how well an applicant will fit in with the existing work team, don't get carried away with those who perhaps share the same hobby as you or those who express similar tastes to your own (in music, for example). The golden rule is always to look for the traits that are most compatible with the job on offer.

Avoid negative screening

Many interviewers are preoccupied with using the interview to screen people out, so that they arrive at the right candidate through a process of elimination. They reason that if you discard all the people who are unsuitable the ideal candidate will ultimately emerge.

While this is a method that Sherlock Holmes would certainly applaud, it tends to put the interview on a negative footing. It can also be too confining. While it is important to stick to the job criteria you have established after careful thought, you should always keep an open mind. However thorough you are, there will be certain skills and attributes that you may not have thought about. You should be flexible enough to consider the candidate who is outstanding, but who does not fit your brief. If he or she is someone who is going to enhance the capabilities of your organization, you may want to consider re-shaping the job slightly.

Don't make hasty decisions

Interviewing sessions can be overwhelming. Recruiters often have to interview anything up to a dozen candidates in a day. It is very difficult to retain so much information in such a short space of time. Certain facts might stick in your mind, but these may not be the most relevant in terms of the job specification. Always be sure you are basing your judgements on the most salient issues.

PANEL INTERVIEWING

Panel interviewing, in which a group of experts question the job applicant, are rarely found in private sector recruitment these days, although government agencies and some institutions still favour them.

Evidence suggests that, like so many selection techniques, the method itself is not bad, but it can be used well or ineffectively. Used well, it is better at predicting success than a one-on-one interview. 'Used well' means a small panel of, say, three people, each with different areas of responsibility for questioning the candidate and seeking evidence of different qualities. Then they pool their thoughts at the end and make a collective decision.

Used badly means an enormous panel – panels of 12 or more are not unknown – dominated by the chair with the other members bored and going through the motions. Presumably it is this mis-use of the panel technique that gives the concept such a bad reputation. There are, nevertheless, instances when panels are used very effectively.

Police forces often use panels as the last stage of selection for constables. The West Midlands Police Service is an example. It employs a recruitment panel comprising a senior police officer of chief inspector rank or above, who takes the chair. He or she is looking for potential. A more junior officer asks questions of a more general nature concerning attitude to police work, expectations, realistic or unrealistic, motivation and so on.

Thirdly, there is a representative from the police union, often a police constable, who tries to assess whether the recruit is likely to be compatible with other constables. 'Would I want this person on duty with me and my colleagues?' is often uppermost in this panel member's mind.

All the psychological research shows that such professionalism pays dividends in spotting good recruits.

The case against panel interviews
Panel interviews still come in for a lot of criticism, however. An interview should be a conversation with a specific purpose in mind. The aim is for the two parties to learn more about each other. When panel interviewing is inexpertly handled the conversation is one way. There is very little rapport between the panel

members and the candidate. It tends to be a series of unconnected questions. The panel members rarely listen to each other. They each fire off their favourite question. There is rarely a cohesive strategy to extract the information that will decide a candidate's suitability for the job.

Critics of panel interviewing also argue that it is stressful for candidates, who can find it very intimidating to have six or eight panel members – sometimes more – all bearing down on them. It can come close to stress interviewing.

In addition, panel interviews are costly in management time and money. Good interviewing practice emphasizes informality in a relaxed environment, which is rarely present at a panel interview. Detractors also argue that if it takes a committee to decide who should work for an organization it diminishes the authority of the line manager and suggests that management authority is diluted in other directions as well.

PROBING PERSONAL DETAILS
How far into a person's private life should a recruiter be allowed to probe at a job interview? In countries like Holland there is a general trend, supported by legislation, towards discouraging interviewers from asking personal details which are not relevant to the job application.

In the UK the rules of engagement for interviews are largely unwritten. Nevertheless, as David Lucas pointed out in an article in an August 1993 issue of *The Times*, some lines of questioning can get an employer into trouble. If an interview breaches the Sex Discrimination or Race Relations Acts, for example, a rejected candidate may seek redress at an industrial tribunal, which can award five-figure damages against the offender.

This is a prime area where self-regulation should suffice. It is common sense, as well as common decency, not to probe delicate areas of a person's private life, particularly when it is highly unlikely to have any relevance to the job.

A multinational company hiring a manager who is likely to spend much of his or her career abroad might quite legitimately inquire into candidates' attitudes to boarding schools and how they intend to educate their children.

They might equally investigate a spouse's ability to cope with a foreign environment. The job-holder is often cocooned against the hardships of a foreign posting by spending most of the time in the work environment. It is usually the spouse who has to adapt the most to the stark realities of living in another country. These are genuine concerns and totally relevant to the job. There is no relevance, however, in asking candidates what their parents do for a living.

6

TESTING AND ASSESSMENT

You have done the interviewing and the candidate looks good, sounds good and seems to possess the kind of skills you have isolated as being appropriate for the job. What's to stop you going ahead with the hiring process? Quite a lot, if the experts are to be believed. Research shows that interviewing on its own is a far from accurate way of predicting who is the best person to fill a particular job vacancy.

Most managers have little or no training in interviewing techniques. Stories of recruitment disasters resulting from inadequate interviewing methods are legion. So where does that leave the recruiter?

The answer is that there is a good deal more in the recruiter's armoury. There is a whole battery of psychological tests, multiple-choice questionnaires and assessment exercises available to the recruiter to help improve the odds on picking the right person. These include:

- Personality Questionnaires
- Ability Tests
- Biodata
- Work Samples

All the above methods – described in detail below – are more accurate as selection techniques than unstructured interviewing (Figure 6.1). Even if you only use one of them your chances of picking the right person are greatly improved. Increasingly, however, those organizations that are determined to hire the best people are resorting to assessment centres which combine a whole range of techniques to ensure that the best candidates are uncovered.

The Predictive Accuracy and Popularity of Assessment and Screening Methods

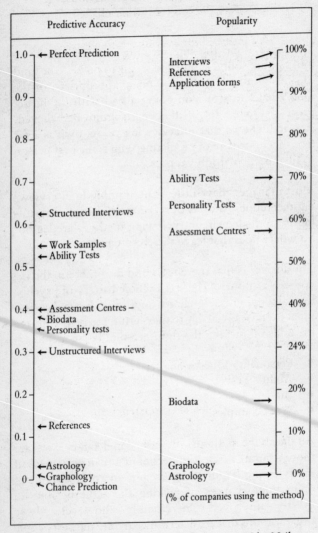

Fig. 6.1   Source: 'Successful Selection Interviewing' by Neil Anderson & Viv Shackleton, published by Blackwell, Oxford 1993

ASSESSMENT CENTRES

An assessment centre is not a place; it is a process. The reason it sounds like a place is that originally that was what it was – notably at AT&T in the United States and in the armed forces in Britain. As the idea grew, so assessment centres moved from a central building to anywhere the process was conducted, but the label stuck.

Fundamentally an assessment centre is a series of exercises, interviews, simulations and tests, which the job applicant undergoes. The individual is tested and assessed in a variety of situations and by a variety of assessors. This helps to ensure that a lot of the biases one assessor might have in the selection process are balanced out or removed by other assessors.

Research shows conclusively that assessment centres are far more reliable in predicting a candidate's suitability for a job than the interview alone. However, many recruiters use assessment centre results to back up or contradict conclusions they have already reached about a job applicant at the interview stage.

There are some competencies that cannot be assessed by interviewing. Technical competencies, for example. You don't know whether or not people can add up simply by interviewing them. Nor can you assess from an interview how well an individual can work within a team environment.

The assessment centre gives all kinds of applicants the opportunity to show what they can do in relevant ways, whereas the interview tends to favour the persuasive extrovert – the person who is comfortable being interviewed. Such candidates have verbal fluency and are usually well turned out. All such factors impact on recruiters subconsciously. They are not, however, the key issues in finding the right person for the job.

In the assessment centre, on the other hand, a variety of exercises are used to give a much wider range of people the opportunity to show that they are suitable for the job.

Exercises

Assessment centres were first used in this country by the former War Office Selection Board and by the Civil Service. They started being used in a non-industrial setting in the United States in the late 1950s and early 1960s. The UK followed suit in the 1970s. Typically people spend one to three days undergoing a series of tests ranging from group exercises and role playing to the in-tray technique, which simulates the typical issues that turn up every day on a manager's desk.

As a rule of thumb, assessment centres operate on a ratio of one assessor to two candidates. So four managers can assess eight candidates in the course of a day. Most assessment centres last one and a half to two days. They give the assessors the opportunity to see the actual behaviour of the candidates – what they can do, not just what they say they can do.

Although assessment centres are usually designed by in-company human resource specialists or external consultants, the assessors are often line managers because they probably know better than anyone the kind of standards and behaviour that will be required on the job.

Before setting up an assessment centre, an organization should have decided on the relevant qualities, and typical behaviours that express those qualities, as described in Chapter 1. The managers doing the assessing must, of course, be trained to recognize those behaviours accurately and interpret them in terms of the qualities sought. It is a very disciplined approach.

Relevant contexts

The other important aspect of an assessment centre is that it tests people in relevant contexts. The interview is not a relevant context. In a job interview all that is gleaned is the person's performance under interview. That is hardly relevant unless the application is for a post in public affairs or something of that nature. The assessment centre, on the other hand – by using role playing, team exercises and such techniques as the in-tray test – simulates the actual circumstances in which people will be expected to perform the job.

The assessment centre can, for example, provide the context in which to test the ability to:

- carry out a difficult piece of analytical and interpretive work on your own
- work on a complex task as a member of a team
- present and defend a case to management

Those are the activities applicants are most likely to encounter in the actual job. A well-constructed assessment centre is built around such activities.

Priorities

A typical exercise might be to organize priorities. For example, candidates might be asked to imagine that a company has set aside a fund of £200,000 to donate to worthwhile causes. There are a dozen or so possible projects. A team of six has to agree on how the funds should be allocated and give their reasons for the priorities they decide on. This is typical of the analytical and discriminatory decisions that managers have to make.

A typical role-playing exercise might involve a scenario around customer service. An actor (often a real customer or an assessor who has experienced the real situation many times in the course of the job) plays the part of an irate customer. The job applicant has to try to calm the customer and deal with the problem.

Fact finding

Another test often used at assessment centres is the fact-finding exercise. This involves a face-to-face encounter with an assessor (or resource person as he or she is often known). The candidate is given a scanty brief on a particular topic and is expected to gain more knowledge of the subject by questioning the resource person. Based on the information gleaned, the candidate is required to make a decision. This exercise allows the candidate's information-gathering and decision-making abilities to be assessed.

It is possible, for example, to observe whether the candidates pursue a line of questioning that is very task-orientated or whether they explore the personnel aspects of the issue. That provides an important clue to their management style. They may display good technical knowledge, but it might be important to know whether they have the ability to convey this information to others and communicate effectively with others.

The costs involved

Assessment centres are really only viable for relatively large organizations. That is why they are common for graduate recruitment. Costs vary, but you can reckon on spending a minimum of £30K for the design. On top of that are the running costs, which mainly consist of the assessors' time.

PSYCHOLOGICAL TESTING

With overtones of Big Brother, psychological (sometimes called psychometric) testing is an area of recruitment that attracts a degree of mystique. Perhaps some suspicion was understandable when its use was confined to a few recruitment specialists or to candidates for senior jobs. However, psychological tests are now being used for secretaries, shop-floor workers and, notably, that most wooed and analysed of recruits, graduates.

Many leading companies use the tests to place new graduate trainees. One reason is to try to get the graduates working effectively as quickly as possible. Psychometric testing is about putting round pegs in round holes. As one occupational psychologist puts it succinctly: 'You can teach turkeys to climb trees, but it would be better to hire a squirrel.'

Psychological tests have an established pedigree. The British Army's aptitude tests were a regular feature of officer selection in the Second World War. After the war, industry began to follow suit.

In the postwar period psychological testing has enjoyed an enormous boom, mostly in the United States, which is very much the home of the technique. At the last count there were something like 4,500 tests in the English language. Some are more reputable than others. In theory anyone can write down a series of questions and publish it as a test. The factor that distinguishes the reputable tests from the others is the quality of the research behind them.

Some tests are written by academics as a money-spinner in their spare time. Others are written by hard-headed commercial people who set out to write tests to fit a particular market.

Types of test
There are basically three or four different kinds of psychological tests. There are *cognitive* tests, which help to assess the candidate's thinking ability. These can be verbal, numerical or spacial.

Another series of tests concentrate on *personality*. These are really questionnaires rather than tests since they do not demand a 'right' answer. Some of them are multiple choice – some are forced choice between two answers and some require a ranking of items. There are also interest inventories and projective tests.

Not all tests and questionnaires are appropriate for selection purposes. So there needs to be someone who is thoroughly trained in the field, preferably a chartered occupational psychologist, to decide the appropriate use of a particular test.

Interest inventories

Interest inventories are more often used for career counselling than for selection. Saville & Holdsworth have devised a managerial interest inventory which gets people to rate themselves against work activities. It helps to analyse managers' preferences for a wide range of jobs. The questions are compiled from a survey of more than 200 management job descriptions from a broad spectrum of companies. They cover both management functions (sales, finance, personnel) and management skills (decision-making, organizing, communicating).

Candidates are asked to enter on the questionnaires whether they like, dislike, or are indifferent to, a particular management activity, such as 'gaining approval for product improvement plans' or 'persuading departments to agree their budget allocations'. They are also asked to indicate whether they have experience of the various functions and skills. The management interest inventory is in no way a test. There are no right or wrong answers and candidates are given whatever time they need, within reason, to complete the form.

Projective tests

Projective tests focus on the non-conscious aspects of personality. A typical example is the ink-blot test, which requires candidates to describe what different shapes convey to them. Or there are tests which use ambiguous pictures. Job candidates are asked to make up stories relating to their interpretation of the pictures. There are also less obvious projective tests that can probe more deeply into someone's make-up. An example is the sentence completion test. Candidates are provided with the beginnings of sentences such as

'Most of the time, I . . .' or

'I get real satisfaction from . . .' or

'I wish that I . . .'

They are then asked to write whatever comes into their head. Quick off-the-cuff responses are sought. Trained testers claim they can interpret the responses and arrive at certain conclusions about the candidate. If only psychological assessment were that easy! The research evidence compiled by psychologists is that such projective methods are highly unreliable indicators of what someone is really like. They probably only come into their own with very disturbed individuals in a clinical setting.

Self-report

Personality tests are almost all nowadays what are called 'self-report'. Candidates are asked a series of questions about themselves, often multiple choice. This, of course, relies on people answering the questions more or less honestly and having a reasonable degree of insight into themselves. If people are grossly dishonest, or have no insight into themselves, their answers are unlikely to be very helpful.

Personality questionnaires are aimed at assessing a number of elements of personality. Proponents claim the tests can give reliable indications of the type of environment in which a person will best prosper – for example, busy or quiet, general or detailed – and how he or she is likely to handle relationships with other employees.

Companies use these tests to establish the job areas and functions with which a person would be happiest and most productive or, alternatively, to gain a general picture of the applicant's personality.

Personality questionnaires produce near-standardized information about job applicants, allowing easier and more objective comparison. They also allow this to be done more quickly and more cheaply than by traditional interviews. Proponents also point out that recruits who find interviews stressful are given a better opportunity to express their personalities.

Ill-informed
While some people enjoy psychological tests, fear and ridicule are also common reactions. According to Clive Fletcher, professor of occupational psychology at Goldsmith's College, London University, much of the abuse is ill-informed. This, he suggests, is not surprising, since psychological testing is more complex and sophisticated than it appears on the surface.

Fletcher, who is author of *Get That Job!*, is convinced psychological tests are here to stay, 'because good ones can quite accurately identify key personality traits, such as whether someone has leadership qualities or operates best as a team member'.

The problem, as Fletcher sees it, is that personnel managers often choose tests at random and are not careful enough about examining their quality.

The worst person to apply them is the blind devotee of a particular personality test. Such adherents are so hooked on the test that they believe it to be infallible.

When the results produce undeniable nonsense, which most of them do on occasion, they will swear by the outcome – even when the person tested can clearly show that there is no resemblance to his or her actual personality.

Restricted purchase

For good reasons, the reputable tests are restricted in their purchase. You can only buy them if you have the necessary qualifications to apply them. There have been strenuous efforts by the British Psychological Society (BPS) in the UK to regulate who should use tests and how.

The BPS doesn't control tests. It prescribes the training and experience required to use them generally and accredits individuals' competence in testing. Nevertheless, if publishers choose to have their tests used by people without BPS certification there is little that can be done about it. All test users would be advised to ensure that they or their consultants have the BPS 'Certificate of Testing Competence' to establish that they are aware of a test's limitations as well as its benefits – and how it should be used ethically.

The results of all this confusion is that some tests which are only marginally reputable are quite widely used. Some publishers, anxious that their tests should not fall into inexpert hands, are keen to control their own standards, which may be even higher than those of the BPS. There are those who would ideally like to confine the use of tests to people who have undergone recognized training. Others argue that such restrictions would limit the market too severely.

Feedback

Another aspect of the professional use of tests is feedback to the candidate. Codes of conduct for test users insist on feedback to candidates of the results of both personality and ability tests. This, after all, is only fair. The candidate should know how he or she stands on ability tests and what interpretation the tester is putting on personality questionnaire results.

The feedback process, especially on personality questionnaires, should be two-way, so that the candidate can discuss the results, provide examples and explanations and know what conclusions are being drawn. Sad to relate that such feedback meetings do not always take place. Perfect recruiters should make sure they do.

ABILITY TESTS

Unlike personality tests, ability tests measure actual behaviour. If people are given a series of sums to do and are supervised while they are doing it, you have a good measure of their ability to add up and subtract. Ability tests tend to be highly reliable because numerical or verbal skills are easier to measure than personality traits and they come close to being an actual work sample.

Work samples

Work samples simulate the actual conditions under which the job applicant is likely to work. For this reason they provide a fairly accurate way of measuring the candidate's ability to perform well in the job in question. Apart from getting the candidate actually to do the work concerned, there is no better way of testing how he or she is likely to fare in the job. The closer the simulation to the real task, the better the work sample test.

There is less room for doubt about candidates' abilities than is the case with all other kinds of tests. The degree of expertise on the part of the person setting the test is also less demanding. You don't have to be an occupational psychologist to set a work task that is part of your normal daily routine.

You do, however, have to be expert enough in the job in question to know good performance from poor. Also, work sample tests don't tell you whether the applicant has the potential to grow in the job (which aptitude tests can), but merely whether the applicant can do the job now. Graduate recruiters, for example, are often looking for potential.

Work samples come closer than anything to the actual job. For example, when a national newspaper invites applicants for a sub-editor post there is a ready-made test that can be applied. The editor simply takes a number of items that have reached the newsroom that day and invites the applicant to edit the material and lay out a page, just as if it were actually going to press. What better way to test aspiring sub-editors? They are under pressure to produce the work to deadline, just as they will be if they are successful in being appointed to the job.

In-tray
A feature of assessment centres is the in-tray test. This, too, attempts to simulate the actual circumstances the candidate is likely to have to cope with if he or she is successful in getting the job. For example, applicants for a managing director vacancy might be given an in-tray of memos, reports, letters, notes of telephone conversations and be asked to draw up an agenda for the next board meeting. This tests their judgement about priorities and provides an uncomplicated basis on which to question their rationale for the way they have drawn up the agenda. They are being asked to perform an actual aspect of the MD's job and then being assessed on their ability to do it.

Negotiation
Similarly, if you are hiring a manager who is going to spend a lot of time negotiating contracts, a simulation

exercise close to reality is an ideal way of finding out his or her capabilities. Often an organization conducting such a test will bring in an outside role player – sometimes an actor, but more often retired business people who have spent much of their career as negotiators. They are briefed on a scenario and play the role of the awkward customer. It would be hard to think of a better way to test a candidate's ability to cope with what will become a central feature of his or her job if the application is successful.

BIODATA

A job applicant's CV or application form can tell you quite a lot about past history in terms of qualifications, job experience, and achievements. It will also give you some idea of whether the applicant sticks at the work or hops about from company to company. Now, a more formal way of linking applicants' past history and their suitability for the job on offer has been devised.

Known as biodata, this technique tries to identify factual information about people's lives which is predictive of some element of job success. The concept originated in the US and in typical American fashion, researchers asked vast numbers of people an enormous number of questions to put the theory to the test.

The technique measured some things better than others. A lot of the early research focused on job tenure with relatively low-paid jobs – clerical and factory jobs, where high turnover rates were regarded as a problem. It was later extended into other areas.

The concept has never really caught on in the UK, although some companies use it for graduate recruitment. It is complicated to set up and some candidates reject it because it is tedious and tends to ask a lot of questions which, on the face of it, seem less than relevant. The link between the answers to the questions and job suitability is purely empirical. It is just derived from discovering that it is there. It can, nevertheless, be useful as an initial screening device for employers who have thousands of applicants to process.

GRAPHOLOGY

Some of the other techniques that are available to help predict an applicant's suitability for a job verge on the realms of science fiction. Among them are astrology and graphology (the art of relating handwriting to personality traits). Although one or two large reputable companies in the UK use graphology as part of their recruitment process, most regard it with disdain. Assessment experts point out that there is no scientific foundation to validate it as an accurate predictor of job performance.

ADDED VALUE

Techniques such as personality testing, assessment centres and work samples provide added value to the information already gleaned about the job candidate from the CV, the application form and the interview. They are simply another way of collecting more data about an individual and should not be treated as definitive in their own right.

In theory the more samples of behaviour you take the more likely you are to get a realistic assessment of the individual. For example, if you are looking at interpersonal skills and you only do it on a one-to-one basis (interview), you're going to miss out on the group process.

When all the data are combined a full picture should emerge of a candidate's real abilities and personality.

KEY POINTS
Assessment centres:

- are better at predicting job suitability than interviews alone

- involve a variety of tests and exercises and a variety of assessors
- enable candidates to show what they can do, not just what they say they can do
- test people in relevant contexts
- simulate the actual work situation
- are only really viable for relatively large organizations.

Psychological testing:

- psychometric testing is about putting round pegs in round holes
- some psychological tests are more reputable than others
- interest inventories analyse managers' preferences for a wide range of jobs
- projective tests focus on the non-conscious aspects of personality
- personality tests are almost all self-report
- reputable psychological tests are restricted in their purchase

Ability tests:

- measure actual behaviour
- work samples simulate actual work conditions
- in-tray exercises test the ability to set priorities
- role-playing exercises simulate transactions such as negotiating

Biodata: aims to predict job success by examining candidate's past history.
Graphology and astrology: are treated with disdain by most UK recruiters.

7

FOLLOW-UP

All your efforts to conduct a perfect recruitment campaign could be in vain if you fail to carry out the proper follow-up procedures. Your perfect recruit, if you have carried out a thorough search, will be a person of high calibre. If the expectations you raised at the interview fail to materialize, your chosen candidate may soon be looking for a new outlet for his or her talents. If you fail to make the new recruit welcome or to provide an adequate induction programme, the impression will be of an uncaring organization – and certainly not one on which to base a future career.

Many organizations these days conduct formal induction programmes, leaving nothing to chance. Whether or not your organization has one, there are a number of important practicalities you need to take care of. These are to ensure that your new recruit settles in well and starts to make the valuable contribution you expect, within the shortest space of time.

FIRST DAY PROCEDURES

1. *Make the recruit welcome*. Make sure you or your deputy are on hand to greet the new recruit on the day of arrival. The first day in a new job is always daunting (especially for an inexperienced graduate). It helps to ease the tension if there is a familiar face to provide the welcome. Try not to leave the new recruit waiting a long time in reception. This gives the impression that you had overlooked that he or she was due to arrive that day and you don't place a great deal of importance on his or her addition to your organization.

2. *Make time available to help the recruit settle in*. Don't squeeze the welcome in between a mass of other important tasks. There is nothing worse than being welcomed by someone who appears to be run off his feet

and can hardly spare five minutes of his valuable time. Apart from anything else, it will convey to the new recruit that you are unable to organize your time properly and that you don't have your department under control.

If you are unexpectedly confronted with a sudden surge of responsibilities, it would be better to delegate the welcome to another member of staff who can spare the time to do it properly.

3. *Conduct a tour of the department and important facilities*. It is easy to be overwhelmed by a host of impressions on the first day in a new job. It is not the time to take the new recruit on a conducted tour of your offices and factory and introduce him or her to everyone in sight. It *is* the time to introduce the new recruit to the small group of people who are going to be his or her immediate colleagues and to point out the whereabouts of facilities that are going to be in frequent use – such as the photocopying machine and the stationery store room, the canteen and the toilets. It is amazing how often this basic requirement is overlooked. New recruits are left to stumble around corridors trying to find such necessities.

4. *Have a friendly but structured chat with the newcomer about what the job requires*. You will have gone into some detail about the job at the interview stage. In the meantime, you probably will have sent your successful candidate brochures and other material to familiarize him or her with your organization. There is no need to go over all the same ground in great detail. Again, there is only so much a newcomer can take in on the first day at work.

It is, however, worthwhile summarizing what your expectations are of the newcomer and the role you see him or her fulfilling. In particular, it is a good idea to touch briefly on the medium-term challenges of the job. This immediately gives new recruits the feeling that they are going to make an impact – that they are going to help move things forward rather than simply maintaining a *status quo*. This helps instantly to bond them to your work team and to feel a sense of purpose.

5. *Get down to business as soon as possible.* The best way to make new recruits feel at home is to let them swing into action at the earliest opportunity. The worst thing you can do is to tell them that you won't be expecting too much of them in the first three months as it will take time to assimilate the company ethos. This belittles recruits' ability to pick things up. It also condemns them to months of sitting in limbo, feeling impotent, while their colleagues are all swirling around them, engaged in a hive of activity.

6. *Give the recruit an opportunity to ask questions.* The tendency when new recruits arrive is for the recruiter to do all the talking. There are a thousand things to relay and a host of people to introduce. The recruit is swept around in a veritable whirlwind of introductions and bombarded with an avalanche of details that will very likely go in one ear and out the other. Since being appointed, the recruit will probably have had a few weeks to think about the new job and will have one or two questions – perhaps to do with pension rights or holiday entitlement – in the foremost of his or her mind.

Give recruits the opportunity to raise these issues with you on the first day so that any concerns they have can be allayed. They can then concentrate all their energies on making a good job of their new responsibilities. If you don't personally know the answers to their concerns, introduce them to the person in the organization who does or make an immediate appointment for them to see the relevant person within the next few days.

7. *Escort the new recruit personally to his or her office (or desk, if it is an open plan office).* Check that everything is in place – that a telephone and personal computer have been installed, for example. It is very frustrating starting a new job without the proper equipment. If something is missing, personally contact the department responsible for supplying it and place the weight of your authority behind getting the equipment installed at the earliest opportunity.

SUBSEQUENT FOLLOW-UP

1. *Check at regular intervals that the new recruit is settling in.* It would be foolish, having rolled out the red carpet on the first day, to abandon the new recruit to the tender mercies of your organization and assume that everything will run smoothly thereafter. Most experienced recruiters make a point of checking at regular intervals whether the recruit is fitting in well and coping with the assigned responsibilities. It is probably sensible to make the first check within a week or so of the recruit's arrival. A lot can go wrong in the early stages since there is so much to be learned and absorbed.

After that it might only be necessary to make checks every three months or so, depending on the period of probation, if that is part of the employment contract.

2. *Set aside the necessary time for a proper review.* It is not enough simply to breeze in and out of the recruit's office and ask if things are going all right. Inevitably, the recruit will say that they are, not wishing to give the impression that he or she is not coping. Set aside an hour to sit down with the newcomer and discuss any problems that may have arisen. In particular, find out if the job has failed in any way to live up to the new recruit's expectations.

You may have made promises at the interview stage

which you had every intention of carrying out, but which you have either overlooked or which have subsequently proved difficult to fulfil. They may easily have escaped your memory and might seem of little importance to you in the context of the job as a whole. For the recruit, however, they may be significant issues – even factors that persuaded him or her that the job was worth taking.

Catch these discrepancies early on before they become a real bone of contention. If you have been unable to deliver on a promise you made, explain clearly why and tell the recruit that you are still pursuing it or that you may have to offer something else in its place. Most reasonable people will recognize that life doesn't always turn out the way expected. The important thing to convey to new recruits is that you care about their concerns and that you are doing everything in your power to deal with them.

3. *Check with superiors and colleagues*. Some modest recruits will not want to air any grievances they might have in the early stages of a new job. They won't want to rock the boat before they have settled in. They may rationalize that any irregularities will sort themselves out in the course of time. But small irritations can eventually cause big sores and infect the sufferer. It is a good idea to check informally with the recruit's colleagues. The recruit may have mentioned to them problems he or she was not prepared to bring to you. You can then tackle the difficulties without the recruit going through the embarrassment of confronting you with them.

4. *Appoint a 'guiding hand'*. It might be a good idea to appoint someone as a go–between to let you know how the new recruit is progressing. This should be someone who is familiar with the work the recruit has to undertake and who has good interpersonal skills. The last

thing you want to do is give the impression that you have a spy working for you who will report back the recruit's every indiscretion. By appointing someone to keep an eye on the recruit you have the satisfaction of knowing that any problems that arise should come to light quickly and not be allowed to fester.

In some cases, consultants from search and selection organizations carry out this role on an informal basis. They act as a kind of ombudsman, bringing to the attention of both the recruit and the recruiter any problems that are boiling below the surface.

5. *Instigate a major review after six months.* A half year review will give you the opportunity to discuss the recruit's progress in some depth. It might be a good idea to combine it with a lunch away from the place of work, so that you can avoid interruptions and give the recruit your full attention. The emphasis at the review will be more on your evaluation of the recruit's work than at previous sessions. You will have had time to make an assessment of the extent to which your expectations have been fulfilled.

If the newcomer has fallen short of expectations, it will probably be partly because of problems he or she had not anticipated, so you should be able to achieve a two-way dialogue that will help clear the way for a more effective performance in future.

This is a time for candour from both parties. By now the recruit should feel confident enough to be blunt about any shortcomings in the job. You should be completely honest about how you assess performance to date. If your verdict is positive, you can use the session to build on success and plan for future development. This will reinforce the recruit's growing confidence and help to produce even better results.

6. *Use performance appraisals to evaluate recruitment.* Most organizations have formal performance appraisal programmes. This provides an ideal opportunity to assess whether your recruitment procedures are working. Recruitment and manpower planning are all part of the same process. If the one doesn't mesh with the other you are likely to have serious problems. One way to foster continuity is to ensure that the qualities people are appraised on are the same as those that feature in the recruitment process.

If your organization is suffering from a high turnover of new staff, it is quite possible that your recruitment methods do not gel with the reality of your organization. It might be a good idea to check that your performance appraisal criteria correspond with the key elements of your recruitment programmes.

Discussing problems that arise at work during performance appraisals can often throw up discrepancies. For example, you may have advertised for someone with good interpersonal skills who works well in a team. At the performance appraisal you may discover that the new recruit has had to work with an autocratic boss who gives lip service to decisions by consensus but secretly resists the whole idea. There is no point recruiting a perfect candidate if he or she is going to be asked to work with an imperfect boss.

Alternatively, you may find that recruits who seemed right for your organization are just not working out. Your staff turnover within the first year of employment is simply unacceptable. That may require you to go back to square one and assess whether your recruitment techniques should be re-evaluated. Are you looking for the wrong attributes in your assessment tests, for example? Are you picking extroverts when you need more introverts to balance your organizational mix?

Perfection, of course, is an endless quest. Like the horizon, it is always just out of reach. Your chances will be greatly enhanced when you strive to relate recruitment to what is happening in your organization. We live in a time of extraordinary change and the system that worked yesterday may not be suitable for today or tomorrow. If you adhere too rigidly to the techniques that have served you well in the past you may well find a serious mis-match between the people you recruit and the organizational needs of today.

Follow-up and feedback are an essential part of honing your recruitment practices. Only by constant re-evaluation and a willingness to discard out-of-date practices are you likely to keep pace with the changing times. If you allow recruitment to evolve in isolation, your management of people is almost certain to come unstuck.

We hope this book has given some valuable pointers on how to find the perfect job candidate. Even if no such paragon exists, at least by following best recruitment practices you should have the satisfaction of knowing that you have made every effort to get it right. Everything else stems from that.

If you recruit good people, there is every reason to suppose that your organization will grow and prosper. Talented people have a way of coping with an imperfect world.

BIBLIOGRAPHY

Anderson, N., and Shackleton, V., *Successful Selection Interviewing*, Blackwell, 1993

Bickerstaff, G., 'When Headhunting is Unethical', *The Times*, 18 January 1990

Boam, R., and Sparrow, P. (eds.) *Designing and Achieving Competency*, McGraw Hill, 1992

Cowan, N. and Cowan, R., 'Are References worth the paper they're written on?', *Personnel Management*, December 1989

Duff, I., 'Don't Treat Job Applicants Like Dirt', *The Sunday Times*, 8 August 1993

Fletcher, C., *Get that Job!*, Thorsons, 1992 (3rd ed.)

French, P., 'Costly Revenge of the rejected Job Applicants', *The Times*, 28 August 1993

Golzen, G., 'Put Job Advertisements in Plain English', *The Sunday Times*, 21 March 1993

Lewis, C., *Employee Selection*, Hutchinson, 1992 (2nd edition)

Lucas, D., 'Interviews that Go Too Far', *The Times*, 26 August 1993

Mitrani, A., Dalziel, M., and Fitt, D. (eds.) *Competency Based Human Resource Management*, Kogan Page, 1993 (3rd ed.)

Nicholson, N. and West, M., *Managerial Job Change: Men and Women in Transition*, Cambridge University Press, 1989

Redmond, R., *How to Recruit Good Managers*, Kogan Page, 1989

Schofield, P., 'Take Ownership of Your Career', *The Sunday Times*, 14 November 1993

Shackleton, V., *How to Pick People for Jobs*, Fontana, 1989

The Price Waterhouse Recruitment Advertising Survey, a research study into attitudes to recruitment advertising conducted by City Research Associates

Toplis, J., Dulewicz, V. and Fletcher, C., *Psychological Testing*, Institute of Personnel Management, 1991 (2nd edition)

Warren, R., 'Do Psycho Tests Frighten You?', *The Times*, 1993.

PERFECT BUSINESS WRITING

Peter Bartram

In every job, writing plays a part – and the ability to write well helps you to perform your job better. Good writing is important both for you and for your organization. It enables you to communicate effectively with your colleagues. It advances your career prospects. It contributes to the success of your company by improving communication with customers and suppliers – and it enhances the corporate image.

If you, like so many people, lack confidence in your writing ability, this book is the perfect answer.

£5.99 Net in the UK only.

ISBN 0-7126-5534-4

PERFECT TIME MANAGEMENT

Ted Johns

Managing your time effectively means adding value to everything you do. This book will help you to master the techniques and skills essential to grasping control of your time and your life.

If you can cut down the time you spend meeting people, talking on the 'phone, writing and reading business papers and answering subordinates' questions, you can use the time saved for creative work and the really important elements of your job. Learn how to deal with interruptions, manage the boss and cut down on meetings time – above all, how to minimize paperwork. You'll be amazed how following a few simple guidelines will improve the quality of both your working life and your leisure time.

£5.99 Net in UK only.

ISBN 0-7126-5549-2

THE PERFECT BUSINESS PLAN

Ron Johnson

A really professional business plan is crucial to success. This book provides a planning framework and shows you how to complete it for your own business in 100 easy to follow stages.

Business planning will help you to make better decisions today, taking into account as many of the relevant factors as possible. A carefully prepared business plan is essential to the people who will put money into the business, to those who will lend it money, and above all to the people who carry out its day to day management.

£5.99 Net in UK only.

ISBN 0-7126-5524-7

THE PERFECT NEGOTIATION

Gavin Kennedy

The ability to negotiate effectively is a vital skill required in business and everyday situations.

Whether you are negotiating over a business deal, a pay rise, a difference of opinion between manager and staff, or the price of a new house or car, this invaluable book, written by one of Europe's leading experts in negotiation, will help you to get a better deal every time, and avoid costly mistakes.

£5.99 Net in UK only.

ISBN 0-7126-5465-8

THE PERFECT PRESENTATION

Andrew Leigh and Michael Maynard

When everything seems to go right, you perform at your absolute best, your audience reacts enthusiastically and comes away inspired, then you've given the perfect presentation!

But success is underpinned by hard work, and the authors of this book provide the necessary framework on which to base your presentations, under the headings of the 'Five Ps': Preparation, Purpose, Presence, Passion and Personality.

Many major organizations have used material from the courses on which this book is based. Now you can gain those benefits – at a fraction of the cost.

£5.99 Net in UK only.

ISBN 0-7126-5536-0

THE PERFECT APPRAISAL

Howard Hudson

Implementing the right appraisal scheme can significantly improve employee and company performance.

Most companies have some form of appraisal scheme in place, yet they get very little out of it. A properly conducted appraisal scheme can raise performance standards, cut costs and in some cases 'revolutionize' the business. This concise and invaluable handbook provides managers and organizations with a practical blueprint for appraisal, and shows how they can obtain maximum benefit from appraisal schemes.

£5.99 Net in UK only
ISBN 0-7126-5541-7

THE PERFECT DISMISSAL

John McManus

Dismissals are wretched occasions for everybody concerned; but unhappiness and unpleasantness can be kept to an absolute minimum by the use of this book.

It tells both employer and employee how to avoid legal pitfalls and their associated costs. Just as importantly, it emphasizes human considerations – common sense, fairness and the dignity of the individual.

The Perfect Dismissal provides a clear and well-balanced summary of a complex subject.

£5.99 Net in UK only.

ISBN 0-7126-5641-3